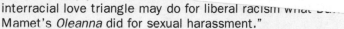

THIS IS HOW IT GOES

"LaBute's . . . most sophisticated complex story yet, this taut firecracker of a play about an interracial love triangle may do for liberal racism what Mamet's *Oleanna* did for sexual harassment."

JASON ZINOMAN, *Time Out New York*

"This prolific playwright . . . has topped even his own scary self in this unrelentingly perilous, disgracefully likeable 90-minute marvel about race, romance and our inability to know every-thing about just about anything . . . The only unambiguous thing about this astonishing play is its quality." **LINDA WINER,** *Newsday*

"Mr. LaBute's real subject [is] race—how we talk about it, how we think about it, and the yawning gap between the two . . . [He] captures the hatred, resentment, and envy on both sides."

JEREMY McCARTER, *The New York Sun*

"The most frank, fearless look into race relations from a white dramatist since Rebecca Gilman's *Spinning into Butter*."

ELYSA GARDNER, *USA Today*

FAT PIG

"The most legitimately provocative and polarizing playwright at work today." **DAVID AMSDEN,** *New York*

"The most emotionally engaging and unsettling of Mr. LaBute's plays since *Bash* . . . A serious step forward for a playwright who has always been most comfortable with judgmental distance." **BEN BRANTLEY,** *The New York Times*

"One of Neil LaBute's subtler efforts . . . Demonstrates a warmth and compassion for its characters missing in many of LaBute's previous works [and] balances black humor and social commentary in a . . . beautifully written, hilarious . . . dis-section of how societal pressures affect relationships [that] is astute and up-to-the-minute relevant."

FRANK SCHECK, *New York Post*

"Will make you squirm in your seat. It's theater without novo-caine [from] an author with a uniquely truthful voice."

JACQUES LE SOURD, *The Journal News* (White Plains, N.Y.)

THE MERCY SEAT
"[A] powerful drama . . . LaBute shows a true master's hand in gliding us amid the shoals and reefs of a mined relationship."

DONALD LYONS, *New York Post*

"Though set in the cold, gray light of morning in a downtown loft with inescapable views of the vacuum left by the twin towers, *The Mercy Seat* really occurs in one of those feverish nights of the soul in which men and women lock in vicious sexual combat, as in Strindberg's *Dance of Death* and Edward Albee's *Who's Afraid of Virginia Woolf?*"

BEN BRANTLEY, *The New York Times*

"An intelligent and thought-provoking drama that casts a less-than-glowing light on man's dark side in the face of disaster . . . The play's energy lies in LaBute's trademark scathing dialogue." ROBERT DOMINGUEZ, New York *Daily News*

THE SHAPE OF THINGS
"LaBute is the first dramatist since David Mamet and Sam Shepard—since Edward Albee, actually—to mix sympathy and savagery, pathos and power." DONALD LYONS, *New York Post*

"LaBute . . . continues to probe the fascinating dark side of individualism . . . [His] great gift is to live in and to chronicle that murky area of not-knowing, which mankind spends much of its waking life denying." JOHN LAHR, *The New Yorker*

"*Shape* . . . is LaBute's thesis on extreme feminine wiles, as well as a disquisition on how far an artist . . . can go in the name of art . . . Like a chiropractor of the soul, LaBute is looking for realignment, listening for a crack." JOHN ISTEL, *Elle*

Neil LaBute

SOME GIRL(S)

NEIL LaBUTE is a critically acclaimed playwright, filmmaker, and fiction writer. His controversial works include the plays *bash: latterday plays*, *The Distance from Here*, *The Mercy Seat* (Faber, 2003), *Fat Pig* (Faber, 2004), *Autobahn* (Faber, 2005), and *This Is How It Goes* (Faber 2006); the films *In the Company of Men* (Faber, 1997), *Your Friends and Neighbors* (Faber, 1998), *Nurse Betty*, *Possession*, and *The Wicker Man*; the play and film adaptation of *The Shape of Things* (Faber, 2001); and the short-story collection *Seconds of Pleasure*.

SOME GIRL(S)

SOME GIRL(S)

A romance by

Neil LaBute

Faber and Faber, Inc.

An affiliate of Farrar, Straus and Giroux

NEW YORK

Faber and Faber, Inc.
An affiliate of Farrar, Straus and Giroux
18 West 18th Street, New York 10011

Library of Congress Control Number: 2006922826
ISBN-13: 978-0-571-22982-6
ISBN-10: 0-571-22982-4

Designed by Gretchen Achilles

www.fsgbooks.com

9   10   8

For Eric Rohmer

Love, ever unsatisfied, lives always in the moment that is about to come . . .

—MARCEL PROUST

The first thing that you want
Will be the last thing you ever need . . .

—WILCO

CONTENTS

PREFACE(S)

I don't have a lot to say about this play—not because I don't like it or anything dramatic like that, but simply because I think it sort of speaks for itself. It is what it is and I hope that's a lot.

Some Girl(s) sprang from a desire to do something a little different: an entertainment made up of a series of duets that features a hearty number of women's roles and follows the journey of a modern-day Candide as he stumbles through a landscape familiar to most men—the mess he's made of his romantic life on his way to manhood. I think it's a great part for the right man, and I was pretty damn lucky to find that guy(s) in the form of David Schwimmer and Eric McCormack, two fellows who understand comedy better than most of us understand breathing. Their dedication to the part has been and remains an inspiration.

I've always been an ardent admirer of the cinema of Eric Rohmer, that master chronicler of the always charming sexual escapades of his fellow Parisians, and I suppose *Some Girl(s)* is my attempt to capture a bit of that gentle, wise, funny spirit on the theatrical stage. Rohmer just seems to get it; in film after film he simply allows people to "be" and then stands back, amused, at the inevitable high jinks that follow. His trilogy of perfect films from the late '60s–early '70s (*My Night at Maud's, Claire's Knee,* and *Chloe in the Afternoon*) remains the benchmark by which stories of love and lust must be measured.

Translation from one language to another is always a funny thing—one of Rohmer's films is simply known as *Boyfriends and Girlfriends* in the United States. After doing a bit of research, however, I learned that the picture was originally titled *My Girlfriend's Boyfriend,* which really knocked me out. So simple, so clever; that one title embodies all that is right with European cinema on the whole and Rohmer in particular. We Americans are full of spirit and can-do hustle, without question, but we're often a ham-fisted bunch; gentle irony is usually the last thing on our fast-paced minds. Rohmer is cool simply by existing and creating what he does; the results seem effortless. Frankly, I admire the shit out of him (an American phrase if ever there was one!). I hope I have cornered even a bit of his wily, bracing, and humane essence within these pages.

SOME GIRL(S)

Production History

Some Girl(s) had its world premiere on May 12, 2005, at the Gielgud Theatre in London. Director: David Grindley. Associate director: Tim Roseman. Design: Jonathan Fensom. Lighting: Jason Taylor. Sound: Gregory Clarke. Costume supervisor: Charlotte Bird. Dialect coach: Majella Hurley. Voice coach: Patsy Rodenburg. Company stage manager: Sheena Linden. Production manager: Digby Robinson.

GUY   David Schwimmer

SAM   Catherine Tate

TYLER   Sara Powell

LINDSAY   Lesley Manville

BOBBI   Saffron Burrows

Some Girl(s) had its U.S. premiere on May 17, 2006, at the Lucille Lortel Theatre in New York City, in a production by the Manhattan Class Company (MCC) Theater. Director: Jo Bonney. Artistic directors: Robert LuPone and Bernard Telsey. Associate artistic director: William Cantler. Executive director: John G. Schultz. Settings: Neil Patel. Costumes: Mimi O'Donnell. Lighting: David Weiner. Sound: Rob Kaplowitz. Casting: Bernard Telsey Casting.

GUY   Eric McCormack

SAM   Brooke Smith

TYLER   Judy Reyes

LINDSAY Fran Drescher

BOBBI   Maura Tierney

Silence. Darkness.

Part One: "Sam"

A fairly standard hotel room. High-end without being too obvious; a resort chain of some kind. Marriott or one of those. Bed, work space, TV, minibar. Probably a nice chair.

A man—thirty-three, fully dressed—sits at the desk and plays with the TV remote just as he is finishing a call on the house phone.

A knock at the door. Another. The man jumps up and crosses to a lamp, carefully arranging the shade. Satisfied, he goes over to the eyehole. Looks out. Takes a breath and opens the latch.

A woman—same age, let's call her SAM—*enters carrying a Starbucks coffee cup. A silent "hello" from both of them; after a moment, a tentative hug. They venture into the room—the woman chooses the armchair, the man moves to the bed. They sit.*

SAM   . . . always. It is *always* the same out there. Bumper-to-bumper!

GUY   Yeah. Yes, it is . . . but you made it. Even with the traffic. Thanks.

SAM   Sure. Of course. (*Beat.*) Used to be a great city, but then, you know. Boom! (*holds up her coffee cup*) Thanks to this bunch . . .

GUY   Exactly! (*laughs*) Anyway, I'm really happy, because . . . well, you know.

SAM   Right.

GUY   Because it's so great to see you. It honestly is . . .

SAM   Good. I'm glad. (*Beat.*) Pretty nice here. I've never been before.

GUY Oh. Yeah. (*looking around*) They're good . . . they've got
'em all over the place now, so . . . a *chain*, I think.

SAM I mean, why would I, right? Live in town, how often are
you gonna stay in a local hotel?

GUY Right . . .

SAM You wouldn't.

GUY No, not usually.

SAM Not for any reason, really. Not even if there was a
convention and you were attending or something . . . you'd
still just drive home after. (*Beat.*) I mean, unless . . .

GUY What? Unless what . . . ?

SAM You know.

GUY No, I don't . . .

SAM Yes, you do. You know what I'm saying.

GUY I don't, no. Truthfully. *What?*

SAM . . . unless you were seeing someone. Illicitly.

GUY Oh, right. That.

SAM Yes. *That.* (*Beat.*) So?

*The man nods at this and clears his throat. Jumps up and
moves toward the minibar. Points out various items.*

GUY You want anything? I mean, like, a water . . . ? They've got
that Evian . . .

SAM No. (*points to her coffee*) Thanks.

GUY Really?

SAM Nope. I'm fine.

GUY I might have some nuts, if that's all right with you.
Cashews.

SAM Go for it.

GUY Even though they're, like, you know, *six hundred*
dollars . . .

They share a laugh at this, albeit a small one.

SAM Then don't eat them. Right? I mean, that'll *teach 'em*.

GUY Yeah, I guess. But I'm hungry . . .

SAM Then you decide. Which was never one of your strong suits . . .

He nods at this, remembering. On impulse, he snaps open the cannister and begins to eat.

GUY Geez . . . no salt. I'm not big on that.

SAM No, you always liked the salt . . . one of your many *vices*.

GUY Yep. (*Beat.*) So . . . mmm, they're good, actually. Not too bad this way. (*he offers again*) You sure?

SAM Yes. I mean, no. No thanks. (*Beat.*) Oh, I read the thing you did for that one magazine. Somebody faxed it to me. It was pretty good . . . clever. Mmm-hmm.

GUY Yeah? Thanks.

The man nods and shrugs. She smiles thinly again and exhales. She sets her latte down on an end table.

SAM . . . funny how you know so much about women. *Now*. (*laughs*) Anyway . . .

GUY Yeah, anyway. So, look, I know this is sort of out of the blue and all, and I appreciate how you might be kinda curious about what's up . . .

SAM Well, I am, that's true. I do want to know that. What is up?

GUY I just . . . look, I needed to see you.

SAM "Needed"?

GUY Wanted, actually, but there's some need in there, too. Yes. *Need*.

SAM . . . and why is that? (*Beat.*) I only cut to the chase because, you know, my kids are home at three.

GUY Right, sure. (*checks watch*) Sorry.

SAM Don't be. It's fine . . . I like when they come home. I just
need to be there, that's all . . .

GUY No, I didn't mean that . . . I'm sorry about rambling on
about the, like, *peanuts* and crap. Forgive me.

SAM Cashews.

GUY Right. Those. (*puts down the nuts*) I'll get to the point
here . . .

*A long moment where the man looks at her, trying to decide
the best way into this conversation. He eats another nut.*

GUY . . . well—I think I'm gonna have some water, these really
do parch your throat after you eat a few.

*He jumps up and heads back to the minifridge. Grabs a water
and breaks open the seal. She steals a look at her watch.*

GUY . . . listen, you're probably wondering what I'm even doing
here . . . back in the, ahhh, Seattle area.

SAM It did cross my mind, yes.

GUY Right, sure, of course—although I do get back here
sometimes. You know, every couple years to see my folks,
that kind of thing. But I'm not here for that. To see
them.

SAM No?

GUY Nope. I didn't even call them, let 'em know . . . I'm flying
out in a few hours.

SAM Oh. Huh. Well . . .

GUY . . . because I really just came here to . . . you know, I
needed to see you. *Wanted* to, I mean.

SAM . . . maybe I'll have just a sip.

*The man hands over the water, then sits back down. The
woman takes a long guzzle, wipes her mouth. Thinks before
speaking.*

Neil LaBute

SAM . . . I called your mom once. Just on a whim, like, a year ago. I didn't even remember the number, so I had to look it up in the book . . .

GUY Wow. I never . . . I mean, they didn't tell me.

SAM No, I didn't ask for you. Or leave a message or anything. I just . . . your mom and I got pretty friendly there for a while, so I was . . . I wanted to hear her voice. (*Beat.*) I thought about calling for you, but in the end I pretended to be somebody else. Selling raffle tickets for my kid's school or something . . . she and I talked for a minute, and that was about it. It was nice.

GUY . . . I never knew that. Huh.

SAM I know. I just said you wouldn't. I didn't tell her it was *me*, so . . . it doesn't matter.

GUY Right.

They sit for a moment, staring at each other. Silence.

SAM . . . it's two-thirty.

GUY Sure, okay, yes. Look . . . I called you, I mean, came into town and contacted you because . . . I just wanted to do something here. Right a wrong or, you know, make things okay.

SAM . . . huh.

GUY Does that make any sense?

SAM Ummmm . . . not really.

GUY Well, what I mean is . . . when I think about it, *us*, I'm saying . . . I get a feeling that it didn't end well . . .

SAM All right.

GUY You know, things end, right? They do, in lots of different ways, for so many reasons . . . and, ahh, we had a really really nice go of it. Back then.

SAM High school.

GUY Yes! Yeah, school. Great times back at Central Valley and a lot of fun, and then, you know . . . we sort of . . .

SAM You ended it.

GUY Uh-huh. Right.

SAM *You* broke up with me.

GUY Yeah, I did. True.

SAM What else did you wanna go over?

The man takes another drink of water and starts to speak. Stops. Grabs more cashews instead. Pops them in.

GUY . . . are you mad at me?

She looks at him, then bursts out laughing. A big guffaw that seems surprising for her. The man is a bit perplexed.

GUY Seriously, though. Are you?

SAM I can't believe you'd say that.

GUY Well, you know . . . you carry that stuff around. I think you'd be surprised.

SAM No, I wouldn't. Uh-uh. I would not.

GUY Oh.

SAM Because I do . . . I *do* think about it. What happened. Between us.

GUY Well, good! Let's talk about it . . .

SAM . . . *now?*

GUY Yeah . . . I mean, I know you have to go, but we could at least air a bit of laundry, or however that saying goes.

SAM You wanna "air" this stuff now . . .

GUY . . . only if it's okay . . .

SAM . . . instead of fifteen years ago? I mean, you flew all the way here to do this *today?*

GUY It does seem strange, but . . . I just feel that we'd both benefit from . . .

SAM No, great. Fine. (*leans back*) Go for it. I can be a little late . . .

The man nods and looks around. He takes off his jacket and folds it neatly. The woman notices.

SAM You're very careful with your things.

GUY Yeah. I picked that up somewhere . . .

SAM You must've, because you sure were never like that when I knew you. Back then . . .

GUY Well, we were just kids, right?

SAM Eighteen. When you dumped me, I mean. That's an adult.

GUY True, but that's what it seemed like. To me. *Kids.*

SAM Whatever. Whatever *you* say . . .

GUY You are angry.

SAM Maybe just a touch. Yep.

GUY Huh. All right . . . Sam, I'm gonna be open with you here. Totally up front. Honest.

SAM That's promising a lot . . .

GUY I know, I know it is, but I'm gonna be, and, well, I just am. (*Beat.*) I think the reason we broke up back then—

SAM Not we. You. *You* ended it.

GUY Yes, but . . .

SAM It wasn't a "we" thing. "We" was when we were a couple, *we* decided to start dating, *we* would choose what movie to go to on Friday night, but the finishing-it-off part? That was *you* . . .

GUY I know that. I do. I do know it . . . So, yeah, I stopped calling, coming over, but it wasn't any one thing that prompted it, it wasn't . . . and for some reason, I always had the idea that you thought you'd done something . . . some . . .

SAM No . . . (*Beat.*) I . . . no.

GUY Oh. 'Cause my mom said that, that the two of you had talked, and—not, like, recently, I mean, but back in the day, back whenever—and she . . .

SAM . . . I never said that . . .

GUY No, but implied it, *insinuated* that I'd led you to believe that you'd done something, and—

SAM I don't think that was the case . . .

GUY . . . and I just wanted you to know, as in better late than never, that it wasn't anything of the sort.

SAM I know. I *know* that . . . I mean, why would I think that? I wouldn't.

GUY Right, so I'm just reiterating for you, then—albeit a bit late In the game—you did nothing wrong.

SAM Thanks.

GUY It was me. All me. I needed to, ahh . . .

SAM What? What did you "need"?

GUY Or "wanted" to, I dunno. I felt, like, at the time . . . I wanted to have my freedom, do the college thing somewhere other than over at Community or maybe just pursue my writing stuff. Whatever. And *you* were a girl that I could sort of look at, you know, take a glance at and maybe . . . see her whole future.

SAM *Really?*

GUY A bit. Yeah. And that's not bad or anything, it's not, but you're just that type of woman. And I think, if I can say this . . .

SAM . . . go on, you're on a roll . . .

GUY . . . history has proved me right. It has. You ended up almost exactly like I figured you would.

SAM Oh, have I, now? (*Beat.*) Huh . . .

GUY . . . well, kinda. (*Beat.*) I mean, still here, with kids and your husband doing what I pretty much would've guessed he'd be doing . . . and back then, when I'm just this scared teenager staring eternity in the face, I could see *myself* with that produce manager's vest on and I suppose I got nervous and backed out of the situation the best way I knew how . . . (*Beat.*) So.

SAM . . . he's not the produce manager. He runs the store. The whole thing.

GUY Oh. Okay.

SAM He's the *store* manager. There is a difference.

GUY Granted. Sorry . . .

Neil LaBute

SAM Forget it.

GUY . . . I am sorry. You're not mad, are you?

SAM No, I'm fine.

GUY Because I didn't want to . . .

SAM I said I'm fine. Just believe me, okay? I believe you, so why don't you go ahead and believe me . . .

GUY . . . all right. I'll . . . yeah. Fine.

SAM . . . and that's really it? That's the *whole* reason why we suddenly just ended like that? Because you had a *vision* of working at some Safeway for the rest of your life?

GUY Basically, yeah . . . I mean . . .

SAM Not some other girl?

GUY Umm, no, not that I . . . I don't, you know. I don't *recall* anybody else.

SAM No? You don't?

GUY Uh-uh.

SAM 'Cause I always had this vague, you know . . . this *worry* about that. Back in "the day." Back whenever . . .

GUY No . . . we were going out for, like . . .

SAM Two years. A little over . . . We were "promised" to each other for two years. (*Beat.*) And you never went to the prom with somebody else? Right?

GUY . . . no. You know that. No, I even . . . I worked that night. *On* prom night. (*Beat.*) It was our senior spring, and after we broke up I was—

SAM *You*, okay? *You* broke it off. Just say it . . . (*Beat.*) Look, I don't even wanna think about this, not at all, I don't. I'm a *mother* now . . . a wife and mother and this is like some ancient Greek history! Why did you have to call me about this? Do this to me . . . ? Huh?

GUY I wanted to . . . I don't know. To just make sure that we were . . . okay.

SAM Yeah, fine, yes . . . we're okay. A-OK. Is that what you needed? Is that gonna be enough to get you back to your something special life in . . . where is it, again?

GUY New York. I have a place in Brooklyn now, but I teach up near . . . doesn't matter. It's all . . . New York. City.

Silence for a moment as this all gets processed.

SAM Wow. Geez, it's amazing how . . . it's all still pretty fresh. You know? I mean, you think it's gone, put in some box under your bed, but God . . . somebody mentions a dance or a boy you knew and it's, like, just *right* there. Instantly it's . . . there.

GUY Yep. That's true . . .

SAM Yeah. (*Beat.*) Guess it's partly due to the whole "virginity" thing . . .

GUY . . . right. I feel the same way.

SAM Well, that's great. *Terrific.* At least we have that . . .

GUY I am sorry about stirring up all the— (*checks his watch*) It's almost quarter of.

SAM 'Kay. Thanks . . . (*Beat.*) I know that you're looking at my face. I feel you doing that—it's a skin thing. Sometimes after a baby your pigment can get all . . . doesn't matter. Anyway, take care. Good to see you, I guess . . .

GUY Hey, Sam . . . you, too. Seriously. I hope I didn't . . .

She starts off but comes to a dead stop. Turns.

SAM . . . I didn't mean our prom. I was referring to the one over at North Central. That one.

GUY Oh. Okay . . .

SAM So? Did you go there with someone? To her prom?

GUY . . . not that I can . . . I mean, this is, you know, *fifteen* years ago . . .

SAM Please.

GUY I didn't ask anybody to that prom, no. I didn't.

SAM Okay. Not what *I* heard, but okay . . .

GUY I think I . . . there was some girl, a senior friend of—

Neil LaBute

remember that guy I knew from, like, kindergarten? Tim
somebody? Him—and he asked me to just drop in with this
. . . really just stop over with this one gal who was his date's
friend. A tall girl, played volleyball, I think . . .

SAM . . . now *this* is what I heard. Go on.

GUY Nothing else. No, we just . . . didn't do the pictures or
even, like, a *corsage* or anything, it was not at all like that
. . . I was more like a, what do ya call it?

SAM I dunno, I'm dying to hear . . .

GUY A, you know . . . a *chaperone*. More of that, really.

SAM Her "chaperone."

GUY Yeah. Basically . . .

SAM And she's a senior. I mean, *you're* a senior, and she's a
senior . . .

GUY Right, true, but it felt like . . . you know, like when your
brother takes you to something, accompanies you to a . . .
(*Beat.*) I *left* her there, Sam. Didn't even drive her home,
or . . .

SAM I don't have a brother. Remember?

GUY No, I know, but I'm just saying . . .

SAM I thought maybe it slipped your mind. So much else seems
to've . . .

GUY . . . I thought we even talked about this once.

SAM No.

GUY We didn't? Over the summer there, just before I . . . ?

SAM No, we didn't. Not ever. (*Beat.*) We talked about
marriage, but not this . . .

GUY Oh. Okay, my mistake.

SAM Yeah, apparently so . . . (*Beat.*) No, I overheard it once,
just a mention of it this one time in the store . . . you know,
where you almost ended up. In your *vision.* I was in there,
dropping off lunch for my husband and I was looking at
something, I don't remember what now, some new thing on
an end cap display—*cookies* or whatever—and I hear a
voice, a woman's voice that I recognize, this blast from the

past. It's your mother. Your mom, standing in the juice aisle and talking to somebody, a neighbor lady or from church, and they're going on about the good ol' days, like women do, and somehow they get on the subject of proms. Of big dances. Maybe because her daughter—not your mom, obviously, but the other woman—her last kid is getting ready for hers, and off they go, chatting about this and that. I don't mean to, but I keep standing there and listening and, boy, do I get an earful! About you, and us, and, well, lots. Lots of *stuff*. And part of that "stuff" is how nice you looked—how well you "cleaned up," she called it—for your big night. *Prom* night. And imagine me, standing there next to this Hearty Fudge Crunch, and I'm thinking, "What night? I didn't have a big night. We didn't go to any prom." But of course she wasn't talking about me. Or us. No, this was about you. The night she was referring to was all about *you*. And her . . . some girl. (*Beat.*) She also said you don't call home enough. Your mom did.

The man tries to say something but just goes for a quick nod instead. Not much to say, really. He glances at a clock.

SAM   I know, I know . . . (*checks her watch*) It's time for me to . . . need to get going before the, you know, traffic and all that. So . . .

GUY   . . . 's good to see you. It really, really is.

SAM   Yeah, you said that.

GUY   Okay, and if you want to . . .

SAM   What?

GUY   Nothing. I was gonna say, if you'd like an e-mail address or anything . . .

SAM   No, that's all right. No. I'm . . . I should just . . .

Without warning, she reaches over and slaps the man hard on the cheek. His head snaps back as he catches himself.

Neil LaBute

The woman exits through the door, shutting it tightly behind her. The man wanders over to the bed, absently picking up the can of nuts. He eats one or two. Snaps on the TV. Dumps the Starbucks cup in a nearby garbage can.

He begins to open a drawer in one end table but is stopped by a light knock. He jumps up and goes to the door, swinging it open.

GUY . . . hey.

SAM Forgive me. That suddenly felt . . . overdue. Just couldn't help myself. So . . .

GUY . . . that's okay. I mean . . . (points at TV) I'm just checking the news . . . or, I mean, the weather. I'm flying out, so . . .

SAM Yeah, you mentioned that . . . (Beat.) It's so awkward, all this, so I'm sorry for . . . but I'm just . . .

They stand there a moment, a curious kind of face-off. The man silently offers the cashews—she shakes her head no.

SAM . . . I was almost out to the lobby . . . (Beat.) This is . . . I don't need her name. I don't. This is so childish! I can't believe that I'm . . . just, look. Tell me what page she's on. All right?

GUY Hmm? What do you mean?

SAM In the yearbook. Their yearbook, at North Central.

GUY I don't . . . why? I mean . . .

SAM Just . . . because, okay? My husband's a Bronco, so I have his . . .

GUY He graduated from there?

SAM Yes. (Beat.) What page is she?

GUY She was . . . I mean, I'm not . . .

SAM Just tell me. Please.

GUY . . . near the back, I guess. Last name was Walker, maybe? Yeah. Something Walker. She was a . . .

SAM Fine. Thanks. (*Beat.*) It's funny . . . I mean, not ho-ho-ho, but still. You want to believe that, at some point in your life, you mattered to someone, that at least when you're young and cute that you . . .

GUY . . . Sam, you did. To me. Absolutely.

SAM Yeah, but I mean, you know. *Really* mattered. Like, Romeo and Juliet–type stuff. And I always kind of wanted to feel that way about us. (*Beat.*) But I realize now, though, it was just a teenage thing and you dated somebody else right after me, so . . . how's that for a wake-up call, huh? Shit.

GUY . . . I just gave her a *ride*.

SAM Sure. (*Beat.*) . . . out on the freeway, just before I hit this exit, I had, like, a moment . . . this daydream for a second where I imagined that you were really asking me here because you wanted me to run off with you to, I dunno, an *island* or back to Manhattan. Somewhere. How's that for crazy?! Now . . . I wouldn't, I'd never do it, but that's the kind of *crap* running through my head since I heard your voice again. So . . .

GUY That's . . . Sam, that's amazing to, I mean, for you to tell me. I'd never do that . . . (*realizing*) Because of your *family*, I'm saying—but it's really very moving. Thank you.

SAM 'Course. Well, so long . . .

GUY . . . bye. (*Beat.*) Oh, wait, hey . . . did I mention I was getting married?

SAM Ahh, no. (*Beat.*) . . . no, you didn't.

GUY Well, I am. Yeah. I'm getting . . .

SAM . . . married. Huh. (*Beat.*) Good for you . . .

This time she's gone for sure—the man tries to get in a last hug, but misses it. Catches himself without too much dignity lost.

He wanders back to the bed and sits. Starts up again with the cashews. Turns up the volume on the TV. Loud.

Neil LaBute

Part Two: "Tyler"

The same type of hotel room. Almost exactly. It's designed by the same company, so the details are similar. Twin beds now.

The man is on one bed, directly across from another woman— a bit younger, TYLER *is what she answers to—who sits on the other bed. They are in the middle of a discussion.*

TYLER . . . good for you! No, seriously.

GUY Thanks.

TYLER I mean it. That's so awesome.

GUY Yeah.

TYLER Married! Holy shit . . . that's the big one, huh? Totally big step.

GUY Yes, it is . . . it's a, well, yeah. A big ol' step.

TYLER No shit, fuck. *Marriage!* Sweet. (*Beat*.) . . . *and New Yorker* magazine, the same year. Movin' on up, huh?

GUY I guess so . . . yep.

TYLER Gotta say, though, you just never . . . you know, struck me as the type.

GUY I didn't?

TYLER Nope. Not really. Not back then.

GUY Oh . . . well, I always *wanted* to write, but I got a little sidetracked . . .

TYLER I mean about getting married! Not *that* type. Not during that whole time we were together . . .

GUY Oh. I think I was a bit different when I was here. Unfocused, or . . .

TYLER Yeah?

GUY Uh-huh. Don't really think I was at my best in Chicago. Not completely, but I feel now that I'm . . . you know.

TYLER Then great. That's really nice, I mean . . . marriage is so fucking cool!

GUY Yeah, it should be. (*smiles*) *So* . . . how's all your . . . art stuff going?

TYLER Good, really good. See the earrings I have on? *My* design. (*Beat.*) I'll bet she's hot, if I know you . . .

GUY What?

TYLER Your girlfriend there, or whatever you call it. *Fiancée.* She's pretty nice-looking, I'm guessing . . .

GUY Umm, yeah, you know . . . yes. A very attractive woman. I mean . . . quite pretty . . . like you, or, ummm . . .

TYLER You don't have to flatter me. It's okay. I already know you like me . . .

GUY Yep. Always did . . . always, always.

TYLER "Always." Now there's a word you used to throw around a lot! A *lot*. Always. (*laughs*) She dark or not?

GUY Excuse me?

TYLER Coloring, I mean . . . you always seem to go for the brunettes. Mostly. A redhead or two, from what you said, but mostly dark . . .

GUY Umm, no, actually, she's a blonde. Well, dyes it, I think, the tips . . . what do they call that?

TYLER Highlights?

GUY Yeah, that. She's got highlights. Frosted ends of her hair that're . . .

TYLER . . . blonde. Huh. How 'bout that?

GUY A little change . . .

TYLER . . . an *appetite* for adventure, I'd say. You always did.

GUY I dunno about that . . .

TYLER No, come on, you totally did! Back then, anyhow. Always had an eye for the *toys* and whatnot . . . remember? Even wanted me to try one of those, umm, whaddayacallems? Strap-ons . . .

The man shifts on the bed—nervous to get into this subject.

Neil LaBute

GUY Yeah . . . I s'pose . . . we did a few things sexually that were, ahhh . . .

TYLER What? 'S no big deal, it's just us looking backward . . .

GUY Right. (*grins*) Yes.

TYLER You had your little ways, like me or anybody else. Things you enjoyed, or wanted to try. Experiment.

GUY Sure . . .

TYLER . . . of course you did. I remember it clearly. Ohh, yeah. (*Beat.*) And don't think I didn't notice a couple of our "greatest hits" in your little story there! Which was *naughty* . . .

She reaches over and pokes the man good-naturedly in the ribs. He smiles and playfully pushes her back.

GUY Hey, shh . . . don't tell anyone!! My editor calls it "fiction du jour" and I'm totally cool with that, because, you know . . . the truth changes on a daily basis, so . . .

TYLER 'S okay, your secret's safe with me.

A moment grows out of this—they sit staring at each other for a long time. Finally, she leans over and kisses him. He doesn't fight it exactly, but he doesn't really join in. After a minute, things sort of grind to a halt.

TYLER Look, I don't wanna force you . . .

GUY I just, well, you know.

TYLER No, what?

GUY I'm . . . I mean, I told you. I'm gonna be married, that's all.

TYLER Exactly. "That's all." (*Beat.*) I'm saying I don't care. Get married.

GUY Yeah, but . . .

TYLER . . . you're not having the wedding here, are you? Not *today,* right?

GUY No, it's in a few weeks, but . . .

TYLER So okay. I'm fine with that. More than fine . . . I'm *happy* for you.

GUY Thanks. It's a very big . . .

TYLER . . . what? . . .

GUY . . . *step*, I guess. And . . .

TYLER . . . is that what's stopping you?

GUY You mean from . . . you?

TYLER Uh-huh.

GUY Of course! I mean, you know . . . I'm supposed to be, what's the word?

TYLER I dunno. I don't know what you're supposed to be. Tell me.

GUY . . . honest. That's what. I need to display some fidelity here.

TYLER Oh.

GUY That's the general idea, anyway.

TYLER . . . you sound like you're really *thrilled* about it.

GUY Shut up! (*laughs*) I am . . .

TYLER Yeah, I can tell.

GUY Seriously, don't, come on . . . this is very hard.

TYLER What is? (*touches him*) This?

GUY Hey, Tyler, honestly . . . don't. You shouldn't do that.

TYLER I know I "shouldn't." I completely understand that . . .

GUY . . . okay.

TYLER But I hardly ever do what I'm *supposed* to . . . that's why my friends have a bunch of *kids* and I have fun! Don't you like fun? You used to . . .

GUY Of course, sure, I do. Yes.

TYLER Then let's have some. Old-time's-sake fun, and then you can go do whatever sort of little wedding crap you feel the need to . . .

She tries to kiss him again—bingo. He allows it a bit more this time. After a moment, though, he pulls away.

Neil LaBute

TYLER . . . you know, after the thirty or fortieth time you do
that, I will start to get offended . . .

GUY I need to stop.

TYLER . . . oh. All right. Whatever.

*She sits back a bit—close enough for him to start again if he
chooses but far enough to maintain dignity if not.*

GUY Believe me, I'd love to just, you know, dive right back in
there.

TYLER Where? (*casually spreads her legs*) Here?

GUY Come on . . . really! I would. But I've kind of taken this
vow thing here, and I need to stick to it . . .

TYLER . . . I see. Okay.

GUY Thank you.

TYLER Then you're doing it for her.

GUY Right.

TYLER As a kind of, what? A sort of gift for her . . .

GUY In a way, yes.

TYLER Got it. (*Beat.*) But if that wasn't the case, you'd jump my
bones . . .

GUY . . . pretty much, yeah.

TYLER You still find me attractive?

GUY Very.

TYLER . . . but it's a moral thing. Or some kind of deal like that.

GUY Umm, yes, "moral," I suppose. Yeah. Or "ethical," maybe. I
get 'em confused.

TYLER Doesn't matter. What you're saying is . . . you want to,
but you'll stop it for her. This woman.

GUY Right. I don't wanna let her down.

TYLER Even if it just happens here, with nobody the wiser . . . ?

GUY I think so. Yes. I mean . . . *I'd* know.

TYLER Well, I hope so!

They share an easy laugh at this one. Her hand on his knee.

GUY I would, yes. Like . . . feel . . .

TYLER . . . no, I got it. Cool. You've made a little *change* in your character. That's good.

GUY Thank you. For understanding, I mean . . .

TYLER Of course. Sure.

GUY Thanks.

The woman smiles and looks around. Scans the room.

TYLER . . . can I smoke in here?

GUY Ummm, yeah, I think. It's a smoking room, but I don't see an ashtray . . .

TYLER That's all right. I'll use a glass.

She jumps up and goes to a tray containing an ice bucket and two glasses. She quickly unwraps one and moves to the chair. Sits as she's lighting up. The man watches.

TYLER . . . you're not a smoker.

GUY Nope.

TYLER So why'd you get a smoking room?

GUY . . . I actually got a room like this because . . . for you, I guess. So you could smoke.

TYLER Pretty sure I'd show, huh? (*smiles*) Look at *you* . . .

She sits back for a moment and takes a long, deep drag. Blows the smoke in the man's face.

TYLER . . . I remember that you didn't mind smoke so much.

GUY Yes. (*smiles*) It's true, I sort of like it . . .

TYLER Huh. (*drags*) Here, want some blowback?

She indicates for him to come close—he leans in and she puts her mouth next to his. They are almost touching. She blows a fine line of hazy smoke into his mouth.

GUY Mmmmm . . . (*breathes*) Good stuff.

TYLER If this was a joint, we'd be flying soon. 'Member?

GUY Sure.

TYLER The good ol' days . . . (*Beat.*) Should I roll us one?

GUY No, that's okay. If you don't mind.

TYLER Wow. Swore off that, too, I'll bet.

GUY A little. Yeah.

TYLER Huh. (*grins*) Guess I'm still a bit too wild for ya, huh?
Same ol' me.

*A smile from the woman. She darts forward and kisses him,
holds it a second, then moves back. He can't help himself—
the man reaches over and pulls her close. She whispers.*

TYLER . . . don't forget about your "vow" thingie.

GUY Right.

*The man nods and sits back a touch. He reaches over and puts
his hand on her face—she allows it, looking right at him.*

GUY . . . I still want you, though. Like, in that way. I think
you're really, really sexy.

TYLER Nice. Good . . .

GUY Yep. Always did.

TYLER That's very cool to hear. Since we haven't seen each
other in a couple years . . .

GUY Uh-huh, yeah. It's been a few . . .

TYLER . . . it's easy to fall out of favor, or just off somebody's
radar, you know? I've known a few men that way—I'm mad
about 'em for a couple months, then, bam! Totally gone, just
these tiny green blips on my screen . . . guys are like that
sometimes. And women, too, I'm sure.

GUY No doubt.

TYLER . . . it's simple to forget guys. But I never forgot you.
Isn't that so funny?

GUY Yeah. I guess . . .

TYLER It is to me. I mean, no offense, but you weren't like some *amazing* person or anything, you were just this dude, we spent however long together, and yet . . . I do think about you. 'S crazy.

GUY I know. I mean, you're the same way for me. Just always kind of buzzing around up there in my skull . . . (*he makes a bee sound*) Bzzzzzzzz . . .

TYLER Mmmmmm. *Romantic* . . .

GUY You know what I'm saying!

TYLER I do, I know, I'm kidding . . .

GUY 'Kay. See, and that was part of the deal here. Why I got ahold of you.

TYLER Really?

GUY Yep. It's . . . well, I just wanted to see if we could talk.

TYLER Absolutely.

GUY Great. Okay . . . so.

The man nods and almost begins, but he simply stares at her. Sits on one leg.

TYLER This oughta be good.

GUY Yeah, let's hope. Right? (*Beat.*) All right, here's the . . . the deal is this. Umm . . .

TYLER Do I wanna hear this?

GUY Yeah, sure, it's no big— What I've done is start to travel around a bit, here and there, and stop in on a few old girlfriends. Say hi, that kind of thing. Before I get hitched . . .

TYLER Say *hi*. Huh.

GUY Yeah. Well, that and other stuff . . .

TYLER . . . okay . . .

GUY Do a check-in, you know? Get caught up-to-date with 'em, make sure that we are . . . you know: no harm, no foul. That sort of thing. No big deal . . .

Neil LaBute

TYLER Oh.

GUY Yeah.

She finishes the smoke and drops it in the glass. Studies it for a moment.

TYLER . . . how many?

GUY What?

TYLER I'm saying, how many little stops are you making? (*Beat*.) You can round it off if you want to . . .

GUY Oh. Ahh, let's see . . .

TYLER I'm not jealous, so don't worry. You made a bunch of promises back whenever, but being *faithful* wasn't one of 'em . . . (*Beat*.) So?

GUY Ahh, four for right now. Maybe five. It's expensive, so I'm just doing the . . . plus, working out everybody's schedule and all that, so . . .

TYLER Huh. Interesting.

GUY Nah, not really, it's probably kind of silly, but I just thought . . .

TYLER What?

GUY Just figured it'd be a good way to start my new life. This whole thing I'm about to embark on . . .

TYLER . . . it's not a cruise . . .

GUY True! "Embark" is probably not the exact word I'm looking for . . .

TYLER What are you looking for?

GUY . . . I dunno. Some other word.

TYLER No, I mean by doing this. What are you trying to do here?

GUY Hell, I don't know! (*grins*) Right a wrong or whatever. Little bit of windmill tilting, that kind of thing . . .

TYLER This was one of our downfalls, I think . . .

GUY What?

TYLER . . . I never knew what the fuck you were talking about!

GUY That is a problem.

TYLER "Windmill"?

GUY It's from *Don Quixote*. No big deal.

TYLER Oh. Right, the old dude on the pony and shit, sure. You lost me there.

GUY Sorry. Look, the thing I'm doing here, going around and meeting up with girls like you . . . is probably kind of a dumb thing. I mean, if you were to look at it rationally, it'd be a bit juvenile. Or fanciful, or you know . . . *quixotic*. But it's really an emotional thing for me, too, it is . . . and so I'm doing it.

The woman nods, taking it in. She gets up and takes the glass to a little sink around the corner, fills it with water.

TYLER I understand. (*Beat.*) So am I on a list or something?

GUY What?

TYLER Is this, a, you know . . . this stop. To see me. Is it on a . . . ?

GUY No! No, nothing like that. Not a big formal thing like a list. I'm not, you know, *Bluebeard* . . . checking the wives off as I go!

TYLER Who?

GUY Sorry! Literary figure, doesn't matter. What I'm saying is, no, I wanted to see you because I felt the need. Felt as if our situation ended in some bad way, or less than perfect, and so I wanted to track you down and ask if there was anything I could . . .

TYLER Is that what you're doing?

GUY . . . what?

TYLER Going around to all your fuckups and trying to make 'em better?

The man looks at her. Starts to say something but just nods.

Neil LaBute

GUY . . . sorta. Sorry.

TYLER Wow. Shit . . . that's funny.

GUY I know, it's stupid, right?

TYLER No, not at all. Totally sounds like something *I* would do!

GUY Really?

TYLER Yeah. I mean, I'd never do it—I'd blow the money on clothes or pot or some shit—but the idea, I'm saying the *notion* of it . . . that's pure me.

GUY Good. I mean, glad you understand.

TYLER Oh, yeah. I completely get it. It's *messed* up, don't get me wrong . . . but I get it.

They look at each other; the woman laughs a bit. Shakes her head.

TYLER Damn . . . I'm glad we didn't end up together. Like, *married*, or whatever.

GUY Probably for the best . . .

TYLER Yeah . . . (*Beat.*) Why me, though? Just for, I mean, since you came all the way out here . . . in what way did you feel you fucked me over?

GUY Hmm?

TYLER Just asking. See, I always sort of felt I broke up with you . . . that you finished your master's and, I dunno, felt the need to go off and become some big *citizen* or what have you, a member of society. And I recall this one fight, screaming and shit on the stairway, but I can't really remember you being the cause of anything. Anything serious, at least.

GUY You can't? Well . . . I mean, we had a nice time together, *very*, but I was just coming off another relationship, if you recall—I had one of the more intense periods of my dating life with you, sexually and all that—but I'm, I don't think that I ever really gave us a, you know, a real chance. So I just don't want to feel that you might be harboring, like, some sort of . . . ill . . . toward me.

TYLER "Ill"?

GUY You know . . .

TYLER Did you become Amish or something?

GUY Come on! You know what I mean . . .

TYLER I *sorta* know what you mean . . . when you're not talking like you're in that one Harrison Ford movie.

GUY Okay, really cute . . .

TYLER But, no . . . I do not think "ill" of you. (*smiles*) Now Godspeed . . .

GUY Very funny! Don't . . .

TYLER Then don't act like some fucking doofus! (*laughs*) I like you. I've always liked you . . .

GUY Me, too. I mean, you . . .

TYLER I told you, I'd start up with you again right now, if you wanted to.

GUY I know, and I appreciate that. I mean, appreciate *knowing* it . . .

TYLER Okay, then. (*grins*) So you're off the hook . . . with me, at least.

GUY Good! Thank you. And it's strange, you know, being here again with you because . . . I'm not sure. It's so all mixed together, these feelings. Of lust and, like, fear and, well, a lot of things. (*Beat.*) It's just, I dunno, some general sense of this that keeps gnawing at me . . . a kind of faint memory of hurting. Of me hurting or being hurt or . . . I dunno.

TYLER Huh. No, I don't . . . nope . . .

GUY Well, good. That's good because I do feel it, in this strange way. I don't know how to articulate it, but it's there . . . some hazy flash. This *burst* of hurt that I've always wanted to get to the bottom of . . . (*Beat.*) That's the deal when you're a writer, I guess. Doesn't matter how much it stings or how *painful* it is for the other people in your life . . . you just can't let shit go! You gotta turn it over and study it and poke it and, you know . . .

TYLER . . . *sell* it?

GUY No. I mean . . . not always. No. (*Beat*.) Well, yeah, at times some *scrap* of life will find its way into a story and that may get sold, but . . . hey . . .

The woman studies him and the man stares back at her.

TYLER Anyway, no. There was nothing like that . . . I mean, I was pretty fucked up most times back then, but . . . no.

GUY All right, good. Because I'd . . . I'd want to know if I . . .

TYLER Hey, you know me . . . I mean, I'm sure I would've said something. Right? So, uh-uh . . . honestly. No. (*Beat*.) I mean, unless you did something to me in my *sleep* or whatever!

GUY . . . what's that mean? I'm . . .

The man studies her, waiting to see if she continues.

TYLER Nothing. It's just . . . (*waiting*) I'm only *joking* around. Geez!

GUY Oh, okay. God! (*Beat*.) Must be nerves!

TYLER No prob'. (*laughs*) Shit, hope she's worth it . . . this fiancée person.

GUY I think so. Yes.

TYLER Hmmm. You think . . . or you *know?*

He considers this and shrugs. She smiles, glancing around the room. A bit of silence now as he struggles to articulate.

GUY That's just it . . . I *don't* know. I haven't really known anything, not ever. (*Beat*.) I'm out here running around the country, but for what? I dunno. I just, with you it feels . . . Ahhh, forget it.

TYLER No, go ahead. (*Beat*.) I can take it. Promise.

GUY I'm sorry if this hurts you at all, but—I'm not sure my being here is so much about us or anything, the relationship

I had with you, or if . . . the "hurt" thing I was talking about, that I mentioned a minute ago . . . it's about her.

TYLER Who? "Her" who?

GUY Ummm, nothing. No one. Some girl. This . . . person before you that I . . . the girl that I left for *you.* See, I think that I came here feeling I did something to you, all this "hurt" stuff . . . but it's really *her* I'm thinking about. I maybe felt so shitty about what I did to her by leaving that I just plunged in with you, did whatever. All the, you know . . .

TYLER . . . naughty bits.

GUY Right. Those. (*Beat.*) Gave myself to you physically, but all that time I was really feeling . . . I don't know. Something. *Bad,* I guess. About her. *Or* maybe the writer in me sees *that* as the most intriguing question and wants to see how you feel about it—I mean, I don't *think* that's it but hey, at this point, who knows. (*he tries to smile*) Wow. I suck . . .

The woman grins; reaches over and squeezes the man's face.

TYLER Well, at least you know it. (*Beat.*) Some folks, they never figure that shit out about themselves . . . they'll go around *sucking* for years without ever noticing.

GUY Hey, I'm a quick study! *Sixty* times or so and it's locked in there . . .

He raps the side of his head—she smiles at this but doesn't say anything. They sit for a moment in silence. Waiting.

TYLER . . . well, that answers that.

GUY What?

TYLER (*grins*) I wasn't *always* stoned . . . there were a lot of phone calls you made in those first few months. I mean, *lots.* To California. I used to look at 'em on our phone bill when it'd come, that same number, over and over . . . and each call was, like, ten seconds! Just a hang-up, really, but they charged you a full minute for it. The fuckers! Anyway, yeah . . . I'd catch you doing it sometimes, right after you hung up and you'd make up some totally *elaborate* lie about it, but I knew what you were doing. I mean, after a while. (*Beat.*) Look . . . it is never cool to be second, you know? In a relationship. It's not. And I was a *distant* second there for a bit! But then you started coming around and so, what the fuck, you just go on and let things happen. That's fine. So, yeah . . . I think you're right. I was not always your big number one top priority during our time together. Not by a long shot . . . and I'd tell myself, "Hey, no problem, we are not that kind of couple"; I mean, you can talk yourself into *anything* if you say it enough. But it's not really true. That shit hurts . . . (*elbows him*) You *prick*. I should've been harder on you back then!

GUY Maybe so . . .

TYLER Oh, well . . . (*Beat.*) Whatever.

GUY Yeah. (*smiles*) I've done a lot of that in my life. *Displacing* crap.

TYLER . . . you bad boy, you.

The woman wipes at one eye quickly—was it a tear? It's gone too fast to tell. She turns away when he tries to check. Smiles.

The woman digs in her purse and pulls out a cigarette. She lights it, blows some smoke in the man's face. He grins.

GUY . . . mmmmmm . . .

TYLER Man, I do not get you. You are something else, you know that?

GUY That's what they tell me . . .

TYLER . . . and I don't just mean about the *smoke*.

GUY I know.

She slides a bit closer. The man doesn't move away.

TYLER . . . want a little more? Just some blowback . . .
     (*indicates*) They're French, so it's kinda nice . . .

GUY No tongue. (*smiles*) Promise?

TYLER Okay. Promise. *Scout's* honor.

GUY I'm trusting you . . . a little smoke and then we should . . .
     we should probably . . .

TYLER Yeah. Here we go . . .

*The woman leans in, their lips nearly touching. The smoke curls
out of her mouth and drifts over to the man.*

Part Three: "Lindsay"

Another version of the same room. New pictures and lamps.
The man is seated in the chair. Glass of water in one hand.

*Another woman—*LINDSAY *is her name—is standing up. She is*
older than the man, nicely dressed. Just removing her coat.

LINDSAY . . . here we go. (*waits*) All right?

GUY Ah, sure. (*Beat.*) Yes . . .

LINDSAY Am I speaking too quickly for you?

GUY No, sorry, not at all.

LINDSAY Because I don't really need to have this conversation.
I don't. It is not necessary to my life . . .

GUY I know that.

LINDSAY You asked for it, not me.

GUY That's true, and I appreciate it, that you drove over here.
For me.

LINDSAY I didn't do that. Not for you.

GUY Oh.

LINDSAY Don't get that idea, no. Do not get that into your
head . . .

GUY Okay . . .

LINDSAY I'm here for me. That is all . . . I'm here for one person
only, and that is me. Me, myself, and *I*.

GUY Okay, Mrs. Bergstram, I get it.

LINDSAY . . . fine. Then fine. (*Beat.*) And call me Lindsay, for
God's sake. After all this time, you can at least do
that . . .

GUY Sorry. Lindsay. I do understand.

LINDSAY Good, then let's leave it.

The woman crosses to the bed and perches on the end of it. King-size this time.

GUY . . . 's fun to be back here.

LINDSAY Is it?

GUY I mean, yeah, kind of. In our old room. One twenty-seven.

LINDSAY Uh-huh. That's true . . .

GUY Lots of memories. *Lots.*

LINDSAY Well, you're right about that. I do have a number of memories about the room, this place . . . I do. And *some* of them didn't even end up in your article. (*Beat.*) It's astonishing to me how vampiric you people are! How cannibalistic. *Writers.* God, it's amazing that you can even . . .

GUY It's just fiction, Lindsay—I mean, what *I* do. It's mostly all made up.

LINDSAY Well . . . whatever lets you sleep at night. (*sighs*) It's . . . what was the name of it again?

GUY Oh, ummm, "The Calculus of Desire."

LINDSAY Right! Nice. *Lyrical.* (*Beat.*) And is there anything new out there that I should be . . . aware of?

GUY Ahhhhh, no, but I'm . . . you know. I'm always working on stuff, so . . .

LINDSAY Oh *goody.* (*pointing*) I do remember this fondly, though . . .

GUY Yeah, me too. (*Beat.*) I never even liked Boston until I met *you* . . .

LINDSAY Really? Well, that's a shame. It's a lovely city . . .

GUY No, it is, I know that, but at the time . . . I mean, me just outta school and at my first big teaching gig, I was pretty . . .

LINDSAY Lost. That's what you used to say to me. You were lost.

GUY I was. I mean, felt that way . . . for a while, really. After grad school. (*Beat.*) Anyway . . . it was a tough first year.

LINDSAY *Only* year.

GUY Yep. I think I was just too young. That was part of it, anyhow . . . way too young to be teaching some grad lit course.

LINDSAY I was only twenty-three when I started here. Dissertation to finish. But still, twenty-*three*. Can you imagine?

GUY That's wild . . .

LINDSAY Well, it was a different time.

GUY That's true.

LINDSAY Yes. A different era, at least. We all cared a bit more then, were all more committed or something . . .

GUY That's what they say. I mean, about your field in relation to history, or on CNN and stuff. The '60s . . .

The woman looks over at him and stops. Studies him closely.

LINDSAY I started in the '70s. *Late* '70s.

GUY . . . oh. Sorry.

LINDSAY Seventy-*nine*. (*Beat.*) It doesn't matter. Has nothing to do with this, actually. I'm just going on here because . . .

GUY . . . right. I meant, like, in women's studies.

LINDSAY We call it gender studies now. Some of us are *actually* trying to keep up with the times . . . (*shifts about*) Why're we here? Hmm?

GUY Umm, well . . . I guess I wanted to see you again, basically.

LINDSAY Because of this wedding?

GUY Yeah, and just . . . I wanted to. That's why I've been traveling around to . . . anyhow, I just felt the need.

LINDSAY Well, that's nice, I suppose. It's lovely to know that our time with each other meant something more than a *paycheck* from a publisher, it is, but . . .

GUY Listen, I know that you've got no reason to trust me here and it's certainly been a while, but . . .

LINDSAY . . . yes, that's part of it. Part of the confusing side. I mean your call came at work. At my *work*, so it was . . . I'm glad I got the message rather than my teaching assistant.

GUY Me, too.

LINDSAY My point is . . . you didn't need to do that. You're getting married—I'm *still* married.

GUY I know. Believe me, I *know* . . .

LINDSAY Then why do it? After what we went through, all that happened . . . why do that to me? Hmm? Risk that?

GUY I dunno. I'm sorry, I thought that . . . I didn't wanna just show up there on campus, you know? I mean, he's still on faculty, right?

LINDSAY Of course. He's the dean now.

GUY Oh, really? Well, that's . . .

LINDSAY . . . it's nothing. Doesn't matter.

GUY Right, but . . . you know, I thought I might run into him or whatever. See him in the hallway and that sort of thing, make a scene, and I didn't want that. (*Beat.*) For *you* . . .

She waits for a moment, looking at the man to see if he's being serious; he seems to be. She nods. Silence.

LINDSAY You left at the end of that second semester, so . . . you probably have no idea, I mean, no real sense of how hard things were for me. There for a while . . . after we were spotted.

GUY No . . . I mean, not really . . .

LINDSAY Well, how could you?

GUY Right.

LINDSAY You never called to check. Not once, not even a *single* time.

GUY No, that's . . . true enough. I mean, I did ring you on a couple of . . . but I'd always hang up. Before any . . . yeah.

LINDSAY We got caught and you . . . well, you took the first train out, as they say. *Figuratively* speaking.

GUY Yeah, I'm . . . yes. I did a bad thing there. Skipping town.

LINDSAY Yes. I'd say that, yes. Quite a bad thing.

GUY Uh-huh. (*Beat.*) I was scared . . . let myself get all spooked by, like, the *specter* of an angry husband, I suppose, and just ran. Ran off.

LINDSAY Leaving me behind. Behind after making *so* many pledges of your love . . .

GUY I did do that, Lindsay . . . and I am very sorry. It bothered me ever since then. Honestly.

LINDSAY I see.

GUY It really, really did. *Does.* And that's kind of why I'm here . . . back in the area. Before I go off and get all married myself . . .

LINDSAY . . . before you get the chance.

GUY Hmm? What do you mean?

LINDSAY The chance to become the jealous husband. The cuckold.

GUY Well, I hope not, but . . . yeah. Yes. (*smiles*) I deserved that.

LINDSAY Yes. (*clears her throat*) Could I . . . do you have a drink of some kind?

GUY Of course. Sure . . . geez, sorry, I'm an idiot for not . . . here. Water?

The man jumps up and crosses to a small fridge. Pops it open and pulls out a bottle of water. Takes it to the woman.

LINDSAY That's fine.

GUY It's the French kind. 'S that okay?

LINDSAY Yes. I have nothing against France. I mean, *specifically*.

The woman opens the bottle and takes a long drink. He waits.

GUY Anyway, it's good to see you.

LINDSAY Well, I'm here. Take a look.

GUY I'm glad you came.

LINDSAY Me, too. It's important.

GUY Yep. I agree.

LINDSAY No, I don't mean . . . not for us. No. I mean for him. (*Beat.*) I fibbed a bit saying it was just for me. All this. I also did it for him . . .

GUY Who?

LINDSAY For my husband. It's an awfully big step, letting me come here.

GUY I don't follow . . .

LINDSAY He *urged* me to see you. Today. (*Beat.*) He's waiting downstairs for me . . . He is.

GUY Huh?

LINDSAY Sitting out front in our Subaru.

GUY Oh. Shit . . .

LINDSAY Yes, he really wanted me to do this. Felt that I needed to.

GUY So, you told him . . . what?

LINDSAY Everything. That you contacted me. About your wanting me to come here . . . about 127. All of it.

GUY You did.

LINDSAY Yes. (*Beat.*) I mean, he already knew about before, all the details from the first . . . so yes, he knows. Now.

GUY And, wow . . . may I ask why?

LINDSAY Not really. I mean, not if you're asking if you have the *right* to ask me, then I'd say no. No, you do not. You lost most of your rights with me when you took off . . . back whenever. (*Beat.*) You lost the *rest* when you wrote about it . . .

GUY Okay. I just meant . . .

LINDSAY Whereas he stuck with me. Stayed in a relationship that I had totally and completely betrayed with a man that he hired. Had given a *job* to.

GUY I know that.

LINDSAY That's what he did, and that's why he is sitting out there right now. Drove me over here so I could find out just what on *earth* you might be calling me for . . . at this late date.

GUY . . . just so . . . so that I could . . .

LINDSAY . . . that's why he is in the parking lot, pretending to read *USA Today.* Because he cares for me. *About* me.

GUY I understand.

LINDSAY And so, the big question now is . . . why are *you* here? Back here after all this time . . .

GUY So . . . I can say that I'm, you know, to let you know that I'm sorry.

LINDSAY Oh. Well, maybe you should run out to the car and let him know, too.

GUY I don't . . . I'm probably not prepared to do that. At this time . . .

LINDSAY No, I didn't imagine you would be. (*Beat.*) That's not why he came, by the way. For an apology.

GUY No?

LINDSAY Not at all. He came to support me. As *my* support. Isn't that just amazing . . . a person who'd do that? (*Beat.*) I think older men are very giving in that way.

GUY Yes, that's . . . he's quite special. (*Beat.*) God, that sounds really bad, doesn't it? Coming out of my mouth.

LINDSAY Pretty much, yes.

GUY I could tell, as I was saying it . . .

LINDSAY Well, good, at least you felt it.

GUY Yeah.

LINDSAY That's something . . . (*Beat.*) And what exactly, if you don't mind, what're you "sorry" for? Hmm?

GUY You know . . .

LINDSAY No. I don't, actually . . . know. You tell me. There's *so* much . . .

GUY For all the . . . what you said. When I ran off—I did get another job, so it wasn't *technically* running, but—took off when things came out.

LINDSAY I see. So . . . not for doing it. Not that?

GUY . . . umm . . . no. I mean, yes, that was probably wrong, too, but . . .

LINDSAY . . . but mostly you're sorry for us being found out. Getting caught.

GUY Basically.

LINDSAY And that's what you wanted to tell me?

GUY Overall. Mostly that . . . and for the leaving-you-hanging part, too. It's a sorta bad habit with me. Running off without . . .

LINDSAY I see.

GUY I didn't want anyone to get hurt by our . . . that was never my intention.

LINDSAY I wouldn't think so. Very rarely is that the reason behind an affair . . .

GUY True.

LINDSAY . . . but that is almost always the *result*. Hurt.

GUY Yeah. I know.

LINDSAY Someone being hurt.

GUY I think . . . I've done a lot of that, in this particular instance.

LINDSAY Oh, I doubt that.

GUY What?

LINDSAY That this was very "particular." Not judging from what *I've* read . . .

GUY . . . I'm sorry, but . . . what're you . . . ?

LINDSAY For you, I mean. I think you're the kind of person who leaves a *bunch* of hurt in your *boyish* wake . . . all the time. I'll bet hurt is your number one by-product.

GUY Well, I mean . . . if you're referring to the story, it's fiction, but . . .

LINDSAY Ohh, don't sell yourself short . . . you can hurt people with your eyes closed. I could tell, the first moment I saw you . . . and yet I plunged in.

Neil LaBute

GUY This isn't . . . listen, I didn't come out here for this . . .

LINDSAY I know that, I know, but it's all I'm prepared to give you. The truth.

GUY Look, maybe we should just . . .

LINDSAY . . . you probably need to get going, right? I mean, that's your MO. When the going gets tough . . .

GUY . . . the tough get going. Right?

LINDSAY I was gonna say run away and hide like a fucking *child*, but . . .

GUY Lindsay, listen, I know . . . you have every reason to resent me, resent how I left things. But I'm here to make amends. Some sort of, ahh, complete *reparation* for all my . . . behaviors.

LINDSAY Oh. Fine. (*Beat.*) All right . . . and how might you go about that? I'm very curious, how?

GUY Well, I . . . I imagined we could do the figuring that out together.

The woman studies him for a moment, then abruptly stands up and crosses to a window. Opens the curtains and looks out. After a moment, she waves. She returns to the bed.

LINDSAY I told him I'd do that. Just so he knows everything's okay. (*Beat.*) But let's get back to this making-it-all-better notion. That deal.

GUY All right . . .

LINDSAY What do you propose?

GUY I'm . . . I hadn't really given it too much . . . like, the *specifics*, I mean.

LINDSAY . . . no, I didn't imagine that you had. I'm sure this is just a big *idea* for you, this hoping to make it all okay. A *grand* gesture . . .

GUY I do want to, though . . .

LINDSAY You want to, or you're going to?

GUY I . . . will. Yes.

LINDSAY Because I don't want you to *try*, it only works if you do it. No matter what.

GUY No, you're right. Okay, I'm *going* to.

LINDSAY Good. That's very good.

The woman takes another hit off the water bottle. Drains it.

LINDSAY . . . and, so, how do we go about it? Making that happen?

GUY I'm not sure . . .

LINDSAY How do you help me, you know . . . get back some of the dignity I lost? A small bit of that back . . . ?

GUY Well . . . I could . . . I mean, I suppose I *could* go out there, you know, to the car, and talk to him. If that's what you really, *really* want . . .

LINDSAY Hmmm . . .

GUY . . . something like that. I don't see what we gain by it, but . . .

LINDSAY No, you're right. It doesn't really even out . . . not after all the time that's passed. Uh-uh.

GUY . . . or I could . . . ahhh . . .

LINDSAY . . . you wanna know what he thinks? My husband, I mean . . . what he thinks you should do?

GUY Ummmmm . . . no, what?

LINDSAY This woman you're marrying . . . you haven't said much about her . . .

GUY Not that much to tell, really . . .

LINDSAY . . . she'd probably be surprised to hear that.

GUY I mean, not *so* much. Studying to be a nurse, and, ahhh . . . you know. Some girl is all. This girl that I'm . . .

LINDSAY Yes?

GUY I mean, she's *terrific*, of course, she's definitely that. But . . .

Neil LaBute

LINDSAY . . . what? She's what?

GUY Nothing. I just . . . I'm not really so keen to drag her into this.

LINDSAY I see. Fine. (*smiles*) She's younger than me, right?

GUY Hmmm?

LINDSAY Younger than me.

GUY Ahh, yeah. Yes. She's twenty-three. Well, in April . . .

LINDSAY Nice. How nice. *Youth.* (*Beat.*) Back then, when it was over, I was sure that was one of the reasons, the *main* reason, that you didn't stay. That you left me. My age.

GUY . . . no, not just that . . . I mean, no.

LINDSAY Well, that's what I imagined. Told myself, anyway. That it wasn't for a real reason, not some reason that would actually *matter* . . . but because I was older than you.

GUY I liked your age. I did . . .

LINDSAY And the fact that your bride-to-be is younger sort of nails it for me. I mean, kind of.

GUY Lindsay, no, it really wasn't . . .

LINDSAY So tell me something—what's the, tell me what you think would be the most hurtful thing you could do to her? This fiancée of yours . . .

GUY Listen . . . I don't even want to . . .

LINDSAY . . . it's speculation. That's all. We are just *imagining*. So . . . what would it be?

GUY I dunno.

LINDSAY So, what if . . . you cheated on her? Even though you're not married yet.

GUY . . . she'd hate it. I mean, what do you think?

LINDSAY I believe she would, because she trusts you. She's put her trust *into* you.

GUY Yes.

LINDSAY See, that's what my husband thinks, too. He said that very thing. That the worst thing wouldn't be what we could do to you . . . but to her. For you to hurt her in some way . . .

GUY Oh.

LINDSAY . . . and I agree. I agree with that. Because it's the other person who feels the pain.

GUY Right. Maybe we should, ummmm . . .

LINDSAY So, I mean, since you've *promised* to make things all better . . . that's what we'd like you to do.

GUY I'm not following you . . .

LINDSAY We would like you to sleep with me. Again. *Now*.

GUY What? . . . Why?

LINDSAY Because you don't want to. And she wouldn't want you to, either.

GUY But, I don't see where that . . .

LINDSAY It's not really for you to see. It really is for somebody else. These someone *elses* that you hurt a while ago and didn't have the guts to say "I'm sorry" to. (*Beat*.) Do you want the drapes open or closed?

GUY Wait, no . . . look, I realize that you're mad, Lindsay, I get that now.

LINDSAY Good, I'm glad that's coming across for you . . .

GUY I do understand that. Totally. But I cannot . . . no. I can't.

LINDSAY Yes, you can.

GUY No . . .

LINDSAY Yes . . .

GUY . . . noooo . . .

LINDSAY I said yes.

GUY Ahh, and I said no, okay? I mean, I can do this all day long, if you'd like, but . . . (*Beat*.) I *want* to do something here, I do, but I can't do . . . that.

LINDSAY You said you *would*. You said you would make it up to me.

GUY I know, I know that, but . . . I *can't*.

LINDSAY Can and will. You *will* do this! Do it while my husband sits down there in our Outback and waits for me . . .

The man takes this in. The woman goes for another sip of water but realizes the bottle is empty.

Neil LaBute

GUY Why would I do that? I mean . . . and you, why would *you* want to? It's . . .

LINDSAY Does she know?

GUY What? Does who know . . . ?

LINDSAY About your little trip here. All these stops you're making . . .

GUY You mean . . . ?

LINDSAY You know *exactly* what I mean. Does your girlfriend know about this?

GUY . . . no. *God*, no.

The woman moves to her coat, takes a piece of paper out.

LINDSAY Shall we call her? It's Alex, right? My husband tracked her down.

The woman moves to the phone, starts to dial.

GUY What're you— Wait! Lindsay, don't! Stop!

LINDSAY . . . then I'd get my pants off if I were you. I'd like to get this over with . . .

GUY But I can't do this! I really . . .

LINDSAY Yes, you can! Yes, you are quite capable of fucking me. You are.

GUY Shit, this is . . . Lindsay . . .

LINDSAY You used to do it all the time, all the . . . every *minute* that I'd let you in the beginning. Back then.

She begins to undress—taking all her clothing slowly and methodically off. Placing each item on top of the desk.

GUY . . . I'm not . . . I really . . .

LINDSAY Always here, in this room. With the red door. One twenty-seven. It was our little place . . . where we'd go in between classes and anytime that we could escape.

Remember? (*Beat.*) The love was nice . . . we were *nice* as a couple, I think, but it wasn't that that kept me coming back . . . it was your promise of a future. This big, bold future that you would whisper to me about, lying there with your eyes closed. That's what I was in love with. Tomorrow. All the *tomorrows* that you kept offering me . . .

GUY . . . I remember that . . .

LINDSAY I'm sure you do. It was easy enough to say, apparently . . . all of that's simple when it is a complete lie. When you have no want or hope of ever seeing it through. Then it is simply fiction and as whimsical as a *fairy tale*—and you were good at it, I'll give you that. An expert at making a usually honest, practical woman like me fall for it. Gobble it up! (*Beat.*) And then a call, one single call from a colleague could make it all go away . . . that courage of yours. Your *bravado*. That's why you teach it, I suppose, and write it, too. *Fiction.* Because it's what you deal in as a person . . . (*Beat.*) The *irony* that I may one day be adding you to a syllabus is not lost on me . . .

The woman is undressed now—she sits on the bed and waits. After a moment, the man begins to undress. Removes his pants carefully. Over his shoulder:

GUY . . . he's not going to come up here, right? For *Polaroids*, or anything?

LINDSAY No.

GUY Not come bursting in, in the middle of all this?

LINDSAY I promise you.

GUY Because that would suck . . .

LINDSAY This is just between us. (*Beat.*) And her, of course . . .

GUY Who? (*thinks about it*) Oh . . .

LINDSAY Will you tell her?

GUY Are you . . . no, of course not!

Neil LaBute

LINDSAY Good. Then you'll have to live with it. Carry it
around . . . like I did. I mean, until I came clean . . .

The man is down to his boxer shorts. He sits on the bed.

GUY I can't believe this . . .

LINDSAY Just pretend we're both between classes . . . that it's
a few years ago and we've met between our afternoon
classes . . .

GUY . . . okay, but I . . . I'm . . .

LINDSAY Shhh. We can talk later. Later when we're done.
After . . . when I'm lying there, in your arms. You can tell me
all about it.

GUY About what?

LINDSAY . . . the future. The future I'm about to miss . . .

*The woman stands up and the man immediately gets spooked.
She gestures for him to relax.*

LINDSAY Shhh . . . don't. Just lie back. Lie your head back and . . .

GUY But, I'm . . .

LINDSAY Quiet now. Just do it . . . go on. You can relax, I know
you can . . . close your eyes and let yourself go.

The man lies back and does what she asks. Closes his eyes.

LINDSAY . . . tell me something. Something you remember about
us. Here. Keep your eyes closed and tell me . . .

GUY Okay, umm, I can . . . I can see us, I mean, recall us . . .
on Thursdays. On each Thursday of that first, that semester
before Christmas . . .

*The woman quietly goes to her coat and slips it on. Puts on her
shoes and gathers up her clothes.*

GUY . . . I was going off to Seattle at the holidays and it was killing us, for me to do that, but I'd promised my folks that I would, and the two of you—you and your husband—he was on sabbatical in the fall and you had agreed to meet him. Over in England. He'd taken that group of students on a theater trip, remember? (*nervously*) Where are you? Are you . . . ?

LINDSAY Shhhh . . . I'm right here . . . go on. Keep your eyes shut and go on. Further.

GUY . . . but . . . right before I left, like the *hour* before we both had to fly out, we met here.

The woman opens the door and slips out, leaving it ajar.

GUY . . . rolling around in the sheets, I mean, no idea if we could make it to Logan or not . . . not even caring about it. We weren't worried about . . . tomorrow. God, it was so . . . I was just *so* . . .

After a moment, the man looks around. He sits up and doesn't get it for a minute; then he realizes. All of it. He stands up and crosses to the window. Looks out. He quietly lifts his hand and waves. Returns slowly to the bed and sits. Alone.

Neil LaBute

Part Four: "Bobbi"

The room again, in a slightly refigured state. A different
bedspread this time, or something like that. New curtains.

Another woman—this one goes by BOBBI *—is standing by the*
window, looking out. After a moment, a flush. Sound of water
running. She can't help but look around the room a bit.
Tentatively.

BOBBI . . . I was just so . . . you know. Unsure.

The man's voice from offstage—in the bathroom. Nearby.

GUY Huh?
BOBBI It wasn't tomorrow, was it?
GUY What?
BOBBI I said "tomorrow." I almost turned around and came
    back tomorrow . . .
GUY Really?
BOBBI Yep. In the elevator . . . I was riding up and, I dunno, I
    suddenly felt so nervous, I thought to myself, "God, I can't
    remember now, which day did he say?!" I almost went back
    to the house . . . I left the paper there with the details on
    the counter. (*Beat.*) And then when you answered the door
    with your hair all *wet*, you know . . .
GUY Sorry, no, you were just a bit on the early side, that's
    all . . .

The man comes out of the bathroom and crosses to her. Stops
and adjusts a lamp shade.

GUY . . . anyway, hello.

*The man smiles and steps toward her, then hesitates. She
looks at him, then turns a cheek and allows him to kiss her.*

BOBBI Hi. There. (*grins*) You look great. You're . . .

*The man smiles as he looks at the woman, waiting for the rest
of that sentence. Laughs. Gives her a hug.*

GUY Thanks. Hey. God, it's . . . hello!
BOBBI Hi, stranger.
GUY Yeah. "Stranger." (*chuckles*) That's a good one. It's . . .
   and no, it was today.
BOBBI Good!
GUY This is it. Yes.
BOBBI Right. (*Beat.*) So, this is . . .

*The man doesn't respond immediately; he steps back and takes
a long look at the woman. She really is something special.*

GUY . . . yep. Wow. (*sniffs*) Is that Dior or something? It's
   great. (*Beat.*) Geez, you look, well, you know . . . fantastic!
BOBBI Thanks.
GUY Really. So . . .
BOBBI That's . . .
GUY You really do. Your hair, it's . . .
BOBBI Same as always. Highlights.
GUY Longer, though. (*Beat.*) My, ahh, whatever you call it, my
   fiancée—she's got those.
BOBBI Oh, really?
GUY I mean, not *exactly* like that, but she . . . just has some
   right here. She calls it "framing her face."
BOBBI That's . . . huh. Nice.
GUY Not as stylish as yours, though. (*he points*) Uh-uh.

Neil LaBute

BOBBI Thank you. (*Beat.*) You know, on the way over here, I
had some crazy idea that she'd be here, with you. The two
of you, and I'd have to . . . you know, be on *display* or
something. Funny what goes through your head at a moment
like this . . .

GUY No, God, I'd never do that . . .

BOBBI Well, I didn't know what to think! I mean, calling me up,
my parents, and then that e-mail from you with all those
details . . . I dunno . . .

GUY I know, I'm sorry . . . but I'd never do that. Uh-uh. Make
you feel all uncomfortable . . .

She looks over at him, sizing up this last comment. Waits.

BOBBI . . . and so I was one of 'em, huh? The *lucky* ones . . .

GUY Yes, Bobbi . . . you were one of the girls I picked. To come
see.

BOBBI You came all the way down here to L.A. because you
dreamed about it one time? That's why?

GUY Not just that, just dreamed . . . I'm saying that I, you
know, I really considered it there for a moment.

BOBBI My sister?

GUY Yes. (*Beat.*) Pursuing that.

BOBBI But we're . . . I mean, we're the same.

GUY Well, not exactly, no.

BOBBI We're twins. *Identical* twins.

GUY I know, that's true . . .

The man doesn't finish this thought; the woman studies him.

BOBBI So, it'd be like, the *same* thing. (*Beat.*) I mean, it's not
like you could've talked us into doing it *together* or anything
. . . no way!

GUY I understand, but . . .

BOBBI Then what's the point? We went out for three years . . .

SOME GIRL(S)

had a good time, some laughs . . . I even thought we had a shot at getting *engaged* there for a bit—I mean, we sure talked about it enough!—but then . . .

GUY Absolutely we did. *Yes.* And that's part of why I came . . .

BOBBI . . . and yet you were wanting to be with Billi?

GUY Not always, no. God, I'm not saying that . . . (*Beat.*) This is all just part of the "honesty" thing I'm working on, that's all . . .

BOBBI . . . oh . . .

GUY I'm trying to help you understand that, at some point—for a *minute* there—I thought about being with her, too. What it would be like to sleep with her instead of . . .

BOBBI It'd be the same.

GUY It couldn't be. I mean, not *exactly* the same . . .

BOBBI No, but, like . . . almost identical. We're *twins.*

GUY I know that! I get that part.

BOBBI That's weird . . .

GUY I just . . . it's hard to explain.

BOBBI Yeah, because it's *weird.* That's why. Guys are weird!

GUY Sometimes we are. That's true . . .

BOBBI *Most* times. (*Beat.*) . . . and that's how I ended up on your list dealie? By your just thinking about it?

GUY Basically . . . (*Beat.*) It felt wrong—when I started to think it through, I mean—so I just figured I'd come down and let you know that.

BOBBI Well, I appreciate that part. It's been a while . . .

GUY Yes. I'm not great with letters and stuff . . .

BOBBI No, not for a *writer.*

GUY Well, teacher, really . . . I've started to do a bit of the other, dip my hand in it, as they say, but . . . mostly I teach.

BOBBI Oh . . . (*Beat.*) I heard that you had a story in something pretty recently . . .

GUY Yes.

BOBBI . . . but I never saw it . . .

GUY Oh. You . . . you didn't? It was very well received. Went over *well* . . . (*Beat.*) I'm sure I've got a copy in my satchel if you want me to . . .

BOBBI No, I don't read all that much. Not anymore. (*Beat.*) Except *X-rays* . . .

GUY Right. (*grins*) Anyway, so yes, you start to make plans, like, all the wedding plans, and your life—this part of your life, anyway—begins to come back up for you . . .

BOBBI . . . like vomit . . .

GUY No! (*laughs*) But . . . it kind of eats away at you as you're picking out a tux and your Cancún tickets, so I figured that I would just jump in there and try to right some wrongs. Be proactive about it . . .

BOBBI Very cool. I respect that. (*Beat.*) And, so . . . how many people are you gonna see?

GUY Ummmm . . . you're the fourth.

BOBBI Huh.

GUY Yes. I was ready for, like, maybe five or six, but . . .

BOBBI Too much flying around?

GUY No, not that, no . . . three I saw. Met with and uhh . . . that was interesting.

BOBBI I'm sure it was.

GUY *Yeah.* One set it up at the airport and didn't show—that was outside of Austin, in Texas—and one, this one girl . . . we only stopped dating maybe a year ago . . . I went over to her place, some new apartment that she's got, and knocked at the door. She was in, caught her at home, but she looked at me, stared at me like I was a *vacuum salesman* and then, in a split second, wham! The door's slammed in my face. I'm not kidding you . . . against my cheek here. (*Beat.*) I'm standing there, moving my mouth in, in, like . . . utter surprise. It was completely *mutual*, our split . . . and that's what I get when I go to see her.

BOBBI I guess maybe it wasn't as "mutual" as you remembered . . .

GUY Yeah! (*laughs*) Maybe not . . .

BOBBI What was her problem?

GUY I dunno! I mean . . . we really did do it together. Breaking up, I mean.

BOBBI No, I'm sorry . . . I meant *wrong* with her. Why'd you stop liking her?

GUY Oh. Umm, you know . . . (*flustered*) We were just . . . stuff.

BOBBI . . . like?

GUY She was clingy, kind of, and a bit too . . . she gained a lot of weight from a knee injury she got skiing. You know, *things.*

BOBBI Huh. Well, that's interesting.

GUY It's whatever. History now . . . after you I'm done and the whole thing is my history. It's past. So . . .

BOBBI . . . and, I'm sorry, but I guess I'm a little slow—I'm here because of?

GUY *Because* you're important to me. (*he smiles*) See, I started by making a list, but I realized pretty quickly that, well, basically I had a fair number of women to choose from . . . a group of *many*. Do you understand? *Lots.* So I wrote down names of the ones that I felt remotely responsible for, our problems, I mean . . . and after a bunch of revisions, I'm . . . I then had to, ahhh . . .

BOBBI . . . yeah? . . .

GUY . . . You know. I narrowed it down to, like, the *finals*. My top five or so. The ones I felt were truly essential. Pivotal.

BOBBI Huh.

GUY I mean, instrumental. To me and where I'm at now. As a person . . .

BOBBI I see . . . (*Beat.*) Well, I'm glad I made the *cut*.

GUY What're you . . . ? Of course you did! Bobbi, you were, I mean . . . you were easily up there at the front. *Right* up front. Oh yeah . . . (*clearing his throat*) I'm a little . . . you want anything?

Neil LaBute

The man grabs a water from the minibar. The woman stares at him for a moment, really giving him the once-over. The man becomes a little uncomfortable.

BOBBI . . . so you never heard about her?

GUY Who?

BOBBI My sister.

GUY No . . . I know she was going to go do that internship over in Europe . . .

BOBBI She did.

GUY Well, that's great!

BOBBI Went for a couple months.

GUY Nice.

BOBBI . . . and then she came back here, to Stanford, actually.

GUY 'S a good school . . .

BOBBI Yes. Got a scholarship there, and was doing her sports and stuff . . . and then got the . . . she got cancer.

GUY . . . shit, what?

BOBBI Yes.

GUY R-really?!

BOBBI Uh-huh. Leukemia and died. I think that's what drove me toward medicine.

GUY Oh, Jesus . . . Bobbi, I'm . . . I'm sorry.

The man stops cold—this really rocks him. He sits back a little, trying to take it all in.

BOBBI She came back from Brussels and she went to school for a bit, but at the end there, when she was really bad, she had to be . . .

GUY . . . but . . . I mean, was she . . . ?

BOBBI . . . funny thing was, of all the, you know, people she knew—she was such a popular girl, Billi—those last few days, when she was rolling in and out of being awake . . . Billi was asking for you.

GUY What?

BOBBI She was.

GUY I don't . . . why would she . . . ?

BOBBI I don't know! I mean, that's what I could never figure out . . . and, so, when you wrote and said . . .

GUY Bobbi, nothing . . . I'm telling you the truth here . . . *nothing* happened. Between us. I never . . .

BOBBI . . . you sure?

GUY No, I . . . I mean, yes. Of course! I'm absolutely sure. (*Beat.*) This is a horrible shock . . . oh my God.

The man slowly puts his head down—not crying but trying to cope with it. The woman reaches out and touches his shoulder.

BOBBI . . . don't take it too hard. I'm just fucking with ya. (*Beat.*) She lives up in Santa Barbara.

The man looks up—the woman is grinning. She starts to laugh. Moves over toward the desk.

GUY What, what're . . . ?

BOBBI Look, I'm sorry, but . . . I couldn't help it.

GUY Why the . . . why in *hell* would you do that?!

BOBBI Please, come on! *Listen* to yourself . . . This whole, me even being here is so *absurd* . . . "right some wrongs"?

GUY I am!

BOBBI You're . . .

GUY I mean, I'm trying to . . .

BOBBI You are looking up old girlfriends! That's all you're doing.

GUY No, I'm not, I'm—

BOBBI Don't. Seriously, we're grown-ups now. I mean . . . for the most part. *I* am, anyway . . .

GUY But, Jesus, that's not a nice thing to . . . don't do *that*! God!!

BOBBI Look. (*Beat.*) You're an okay guy, I liked you a lot back however many years ago, so I don't want this other memory—this thing you're doing here—to be the last image I have of you. I don't.

GUY I just wanted to say that I've really been thinking about this and that I wanted to see you, to look in your face and to tell you—

BOBBI So *see* me, then, talk to me . . . ask for my sister's number, shit, I do not care! But don't go and do some pathetic thing like *pretending* to smooth things over, as if you're just dying inside to make it all good between us . . .

GUY I'm not! I mean, I am, but . . .

BOBBI Don't do that.

GUY I really *do* want to . . . (*softer*) I *do*, Bobbi . . . I've always wanted to . . .

They stand for a moment, facing each other. The woman relaxes against the desk as the man stares at her. A slight movement.

BOBBI . . . this is *not* one of those moments where I'm really hoping that you'll kiss me, okay?

GUY . . . I *know* . . .

The man backs up a bit, just to give her a little space.

GUY . . . what I was trying to do in this case was to let you know that I never did that, went after your sister, or anybody else, for that matter . . . because I liked you so much. Respected you.

BOBBI I see. And . . . did you lose respect for me when you got out there to Chicago or something? All that *respect* you had for me . . . ?

GUY . . . no, not at all!

BOBBI Then how come I didn't hear from you or anything? That part I never could quite . . . you just took off . . .

GUY I . . . because I was . . . (*Beat.*) I met someone.

BOBBI Oh.

GUY Yes. I met this other, sort of hooked up with another girl out there and, well, you know how I feel about the whole *monogamy* thing, so . . .

BOBBI But . . . you were supposed to be being monogamous with *me.* Then.

GUY Right, but . . .

BOBBI So how come you went off with her? Who was she that you'd start a . . . ?

GUY Just a girl. Some girl, that's all.

BOBBI "Some girl" that you . . .

GUY . . . yes. That I did that to you with. (*Beat.*) It was a mistake. I have a little bit of a *history* there. Doing that kinda thing.

BOBBI Okay. See . . . now I get it. After all this time. I *now* get what one phone call would've taken care of . . .

GUY I should've called you or . . . called. I started to, *dozens* of times, but I . . .

BOBBI . . . that would've helped . . .

GUY . . . I kept hanging up. I'd ring you but then I'd chicken out. (*Beat.*) I didn't want you to not like me.

BOBBI But you didn't really want me to like you, though, either. True?

GUY Sorta. It was complicated . . .

BOBBI So you *sorta* just disappeared on me there. I mean, I figured it out, that you must've, but . . .

GUY . . . I went with the "clean break." I didn't want to muddy it up with a bunch of *talk*.

BOBBI I see. Okay . . . (*Beat.*) Well, we're probably done here, aren't we?

GUY What? No . . . we're just getting started. Bobbi, you don't understand. I can't go forward in my . . . whatever, life or

love or, I mean, *any* of that without first . . . you know . . .
(*Beat*.) For us to . . . giving ourselves a chance to . . . to . . .
I don't know . . .

*The woman suddenly stops and digs in her purse. She pulls out
an envelope and holds it out toward the man.*

BOBBI Here. It's a gift certificate. For Williams-Sonoma.
GUY Huh? . . .
BOBBI You said you're registered there . . .
GUY No, I can't accept a . . .
BOBBI Look, don't be an asshole about this, *too*, okay? Just
take it.

*The woman moves straight toward him; he backs up. She takes
the envelope and shoves it into his shirt pocket.*

*The man reaches for her arm and holds it, trying hard to pull
her close and explain.*

The woman remains where she is. Stares hard at him.

GUY Bobbi, please don't let a misunderstanding from the
past—this sort of rotten behavior on my side—ruin our
reunion here! (*Beat*.) I do feel bad about what I did to
you . . . my *part* in all that, but—
BOBBI Which *part*? The fantasies about my sister or the
dumping-me-for-some-other-girl-at-random stuff? Huh?!
GUY Prob'ly all of it. You're right. I mean, if I really . . .
BOBBI What?
GUY If I was to really examine it, to really *really* get down to
the . . .
BOBBI . . . but you never *really* do, do you? The work, I mean.
Not ever.
GUY Well, yeah, I . . .

BOBBI No, you don't. Not now. Not then.

GUY . . . what's this if it's not me trying to . . . ?

BOBBI This isn't work. Oh, no. Not what you're doing here . . .

GUY Don't say that. I'm trying to—

BOBBI . . . you're making sure you haven't missed out on something! That is *exactly* what you're doing!!!

GUY No, I—I'm . . .

BOBBI Yes, you wanna know that this nurse of yours—isn't that what you've said she studies?—that she's the best deal you can get. The nicest, the sweetest, the *prettiest* of the—

GUY No, that's not true, I'm—

BOBBI Bullshit. Bull*shit*! I *know* you. Man, I'd love to just . . .

GUY . . . what? . . .

BOBBI I would *love* to know how many you actually had there, on your "list" thingie. Seriously. How many girls? How *many*? I'll bet the sum total was pretty staggering . . .

GUY You think whatever you want . . .

BOBBI Oh, I will.

GUY Go ahead, do.

BOBBI I *do* and I'm going to!

GUY Fine!! (*Beat.*) God . . . we can at least be *civilized* about this, can't we? I mean, Jesus, even if we just end up as, you know . . . as . . .

BOBBI . . . "friends"? You were not just about to say that, were you? Huh?

GUY . . . no . . .

BOBBI God, I hope not . . .

GUY I just—

BOBBI Because I don't need any friends. Okay? Or, I guess I should be more specific here . . . I do not need *you*.

GUY Well, that's not very nice . . .

BOBBI I wasn't trying to be *nice*. At all. I'm serious . . . why would I want to be pals with you? Buddies? Especially *now*. Hmm? I mean, I barely wanted to *see* you! (*Beat.*) God, you always were this grandiose guy, but I had no idea—really, not until *this* moment—that it might actually be pathological. So, no—I think "friends" is off the list.

GUY But, I . . . *shit!* Bobbi, look, I'm . . . I always *meant* well.

BOBBI Fuck you. (*Beat.*) That is *pathetic*. Oppenheimer meant well. Pol Pot *meant* well. It's not about the meaning, it's about the doing. Guys always *mean* well—right before they fuck somebody over . . .

GUY Oh, come *on* . . .

BOBBI What?

GUY I mean, please, that is not . . .

BOBBI Not what? You think it's okay as long as it's just one person, rather than a dozen? Or a million? When is *hurting* okay? When *you* say so, or is it just open season, all of us going at it in any way we see fit?

GUY Look, I'm not saying it's all right to . . .

BOBBI Seriously, if you've got the answer, tell me . . .

GUY . . . but you can't, you *cannot* equate like, some *war* with me not calling you!

BOBBI Why not? Who says I can't? In fact, I already did. Just now, and I'm gonna stand by it. I am, because when you do what you do, what it sounds like you've done—a *lot*—people get hurt. Injured. A bit of them, some piece . . . it dies. They lose something that will never come back. Not *ever*. This *part* that you decide you can just . . . take from them and damage. Piss on.

GUY I, I didn't take anything from . . .

BOBBI You did! From me you *did*—not what you thought maybe, but you did do that—and you didn't care. You did not even look back, and *that* . . . that one little brutal gesture . . . makes you more than just some ex-boyfriend. You are like a killer. An assassin. Some emotional *terrorist* who's . . . (*Beat.*) No, you know what the truth is? This—all this stuff that you do—just makes you a not-very-nice person. And that is as bad as it gets, far as I'm concerned—

The woman moves toward the door. The man follows closely.

GUY Bobbi, this is not what I wanted, I mean, hoped to happen here . . .
BOBBI Well, then. Surprise . . .

The woman starts to walk out. The man hurries ahead of her and blocks the way.

GUY Wai, wai, wait . . . just wait a second! Please don't leave! Look, I ran away and all that shit, yes, I know that, but I *did* look back! I've been searching for a way back ever since. Bobbi, my *entire* life since knowing you has been devoted to finding someone like you . . . It's *so* obvious now! Look! Here.

The man pulls out his wallet. Holds up a photo toward her. She takes the wallet and studies the photo.

BOBBI . . . she's pretty.
GUY No, thanks, but, no . . . what I mean is, a little similar, huh? Yeah. She's even in medicine . . . I've been deluding myself all this time. What we had—*have*—what there is between us, it's *undeniable*.
BOBBI . . . you're sure you don't mean my *sister*?
GUY Come on! Please . . . Bobbi . . .

The woman reaches over and hands back his wallet. Waits.

BOBBI Why didn't you come back then? I mean, before this? *Why?*

GUY Okay, yes, that's an *excellent* question. Right! Or, Jesus, here's one for you, Why'd I ever leave in the first place? Huh? I applied to UCLA for postgrad *and* I got in—you didn't know that, did you?—no, you didn't because I *lied* to you about it . . . tore up the letter and said I "had" to go to Chicago, Northwestern was the only place for me . . . why?! Why do people do shit of that nature, such blatant, foolish shit that ruins our lives? I dunno, that's the answer. I do not. I can only speak for me, and the truth of it is . . . I just wasn't ready. The best thing in my life comes up to me in the student union one day and sits down across from me with her lunch . . . I'm *twenty-two* years old! That's my only defense. I was a kid and I . . . Bobbi, I fucked up. I . . .

BOBBI God . . . that's, I don't . . . no, I can't accept that.

GUY What? I'm—

BOBBI I'm sorry, but . . .

GUY . . . it's the *truth*!

BOBBI I don't care! It's too easy, too . . . no. *No.*

The woman tries to push past him but the man grabs on, holds her tight. She struggles and they go down to the floor. Hard. She tries to crawl away but he holds on.

BOBBI Don't! Stop it!! Don't do some last-ditch, shitty thing that we'll both be sorry for . . .

GUY No, *please!* Just hold up! Listen to me for a moment. Really, don't do that, walk out and . . .

The woman tears at him as she gets to her feet, backs into a lamp and knocks it over. A microphone on a cord drops out of the shade, dangling there. Silence.

BOBBI . . . I hope that's for your iPod.

GUY Bobbi, look, I . . .

BOBBI What the hell is that? Hmm?

GUY It's a . . . this is just . . . a mike.

BOBBI "Mike"? Like a *microphone?!* Why is there a . . . ? Why?!

GUY . . . it's . . . because I'm . . .

BOBBI . . . are you *taping* this? What we're saying to each other?! Huh?!

GUY Yes! Yes, I am taping our . . . but it is not a . . . Bobbi, I'm . . .

BOBBI Why? *Why* would you do that? (*Pulls away*) *Stop!* I'll sit here while you explain. I will. Go ahead . . . try.

The man stands slowly, gathers himself, tries to tuck his ripped shirt back into his pants.

GUY Listen . . . I had this thought . . . just a sort of crazy notion about my . . . You said you never read my story, that was in the . . . for *years* I've tried to write, you know, while I'm off teaching . . . and then suddenly I found my voice. I did. In my own romantic *foibles!* (*tries to laugh*) See, and now, all of a sudden, I'm an *author* and respected and, you know, I got this taste of, this *minor* taste of some celebrity. Okay? So I was, I just thought, you know, what the hell, I'd keep doing it; I approached *Esquire* and they're interested, so I started taping all these different—but that's not why I came here. It *isn't*. What I said about seeing you again is true, all my feelings for you. Completely.

BOBBI Yeah? Really?

GUY Yes. Absolutely!

The woman stands and straightens her clothing. Stares at him.

BOBBI Well, that's great—thank God you'd never make me feel "all uncomfortable." You are *un*believable!

Neil LaBute

The woman steps toward the door but the man holds up a hand.

GUY Wait! Look, please . . . I know this seems bad, I *know*
that, but I just wanna say a few things here, and if you think
they're crap or, like, ummmm, too sentimental, or whatever
. . . then walk out and slam the door right in my face. Totally
understood. But just gimme a break, hear me out . . .

*The woman doesn't verbally agree; she simply stops where she
is. Even backs up a touch. He has the floor.*

GUY All right, good, okay then . . . first off, yes, I have done a
handful of, like . . . wrongs in my life. Twisted a few truths to
get what I wanted, or at least thought I wanted, yes. I've
done that and more . . . hell, I even put some of it down in
black and white and didn't give a shit that somebody might
get hurt because of it! Okay. Guilty as charged. (*Beat.*) I
really do believe this stuff is mine, though, once it
happens—it's out there in the atmosphere and if I wanna use
it, or alter it a bit to expose a greater truth . . . who's to say
that's wrong? Hmm? *Who?*

The man looks over to see how this is going down. Undecided.

GUY Now . . . I acknowledge that you may disagree with that,
may feel that what I do is pornography almost . . . but either
way, whether I'm a shit or a fearless *cartographer* of the
soul—I mean, I've had reviews that say that very thing. I
have—no one is in any way exempt from screwing up once in
a while, I don't care who you are! So, okay, I've done that, a
host of things that—if ya *nitpick*—absolutely, they look awful
stacked up end on end. But . . .

*The man stops, tries to figure out exactly where he's going
with this—he's doing well now, but he needs an ending.*

GUY I really did need to see you again.

BOBBI Yeah, and maybe even make a buck or two off of it.

GUY Fine, yes, you got me! You smoked me out, so bully for you. I sometimes use the people around me to further my career . . . well, Bobbi, that makes me an American, frankly, and that is about it. Look, I'm not even one of these authors who're out there right now pretending like all their shit is real or, or . . . hiding behind the persona of some twelve-year-old *boy*—I don't do any of that! I am just me and I write amusing stories while changing the names of everybody involved and I don't see who's getting hurt by it. I really don't. (*Beat.*) I'm not, like, you know . . . doing this all *haphazardly* or anything. It's, it's . . . for *Esquire*! Just because I'm an author doesn't mean I'm not able to have human . . . *stuff*. I can't help it if I'm complex. (*Beat.*) Does that make me some big, despicable creature just because I continue to search? To reach out for my happiness on a profoundly human level? I don't think so. I'm not sick, Bobbi. I am not evil. I may be a bunch of things, but I'm not that . . . And I'm not trying to take anything away from what I did, I am not—I did such a . . . stupid, stupid thing back so many years ago, and I'm *sorry*. I could try and place blame on something else, say it's a horrible age we live in now, a world that doesn't give two shits about other people's feelings and where folks sit up until *four* in the morning searching for sex on the Internet while a loved one is sleeping fifty feet away . . . or some guy will *text-message* his wife to say "I'm leaving you." All of these little atrocities that we visit on each other that are really pretty breathtaking. (*Beat.*) But I can't. That's not the problem. *This* was my fault, all of it. I was just young and dumb and, I dunno, goofy and, you know—those were my *good* qualities! . . . I'm a guy, I'm bad at this, Bobbi; I found the single greatest person I could ever imagine being near, I mean *standing* near, even, and she liked me. Me! And that just

didn't compute, it did not make sense, no matter what she
said to me . . . so I made myself believe it wasn't true and I
ran off. Like some three-year-old. (*Beat.*) But I've grown up
since then, I have—all this being with other women and
writing about it and telling myself that I should go visit my
past before I marry . . . I realize now, it's all about *you*! I
don't care if you buy it or hate me or laugh in my face . . .
(*tears up a bit*) I love you and I'm . . . ohh, boy. No way I'm
gonna top that, so I'll just leave off right there. I *love* you,
Bobbi. Not your sister, not anybody else I've ever known,
even this girl I'm supposed to marry . . . no one. Just you.

*The man stops now and waits—the woman doesn't even
blink.*

GUY . . . I wish you'd say something.
BOBBI It's very late.
GUY O-kay . . . is that *metaphoric*, or . . . ?
BOBBI I think sort of all-encompassing. (*glances at her watch*)
    It's late.
GUY Yeah, but we could . . . what're you saying here? I'm . . .
BOBBI Nothing. I have to go. (*points*) It's for fifty dollars.

*The woman steps around the man and goes to the door. Exits.
The man stands for a long while. Frozen in place.*

*Finally he moves over near the lamp, opens a drawer, and pulls
out a small tape player. Clicks it to Off. The man presses Play
and listens to a snippet of conversation with Bobbi. He presses
Stop and takes the tape out of the machine. The man begins to
pull the tape from the cassette casing. A long spool of brown
spills out of it.*

*After a moment, the phone rings. The man crosses to the desk
and answers the phone.*

GUY . . . Hello? Hey, hi. Good. No, I'm fine, yeah. Yes. Work was
good. How was your class? . . . (*Beat.*) Uh-huh . . . no, yeah,
it's a beautiful day, little windy, but lovely . . . really. Well,
I've told you how L.A. can be, right? It's great one minute,
and then the next is like, well, yeah: great. But a different
kind of great. *Great-er.* (*laughs*) Hey, honey, guess what? I
think I'll catch a red-eye back after my next . . . no, tonight.
Why? Well, because I miss you. That's why . . .

*As he speaks into the receiver, he retrieves a pencil and begins
the slow process of winding the tape back into the case—
carefully, inch by inch.*

GUY And love you, too. Yes! Love you so much. I do. I love you
very much. Very, very much . . . and always will. Yes. I
promise. Uh-huh. Will always and always and always . . .
yes, and always more. *Always* . . .

Silence. Darkness.

AFTERWORD(S): "DELETED SCENE"

It's a funny thing to look at a play again and reconsider it after a successful run—some people might think one should leave well enough alone and move on, but I'm funny that way. I'm funny about a lot of things, actually, but this one in particular: I can't help tinkering with my work. And so it goes with the text of *Some Girl(s)*.

This script went through a fairly healthy round of changes during its London run in the spring of 2005, even though, due to time restrictions, the version published in England doesn't reflect that. If anything, what you have in your hands right now is closer to what ended up being printed there. What played onstage, however, was a more streamlined and somewhat simpler tale of a man who travels back into his life to honestly try to find something of worth in the wreckage of his past relationships. The original text, though, had a parallel story of journalistic opportunism running alongside the more romantic elements, which we ultimately trimmed out of that first production. This was partly driven by pragmatic concerns— we wanted an intermissionless show to keep things moving dramatically—and partly a result of dramaturgical choices made by the director, the actors, and myself.

Time is probably what brings that side of the story back now; recent events in American publishing—from the latest revelations of James Frey to the "unmasking" of JT LeRoy to the always entertaining, frustrating questions that the First

Amendment brings to light (specifically, how much literary freedom should one person be allowed to enjoy when another person's life is directly, and perhaps adversely, affected?)— have made those elements much more viable and interesting, and so the director Jo Bonney and I decided to reinstate the more duplicitous nature of *Some Girl(s)*. I'm certainly no stranger to characters who hide and lie and fib their way through a hundred pages or so; trying to help a character negotiate the difficult waters of actually caring for the very people he's about to knowingly hurt, however, was something new and an exciting challenge for me as a writer. The first version of *Some Girl(s)* shows a man making casual blunders in his relationships; this edition tracks a more ruthless romantic terrorist.

What follows is the theatrical equivalent of a DVD extra—an additional scene for the play, written between that first London run and the U.S. premiere, which has yet to find a home in a production of the play, even though the scene's existence has certainly contributed to the story's evolution. I'm still not exactly certain why the character of Reggie exists. The idea simply struck me for another movement and I put the thing down on paper in one long burst of writing. It didn't come from a feeling that the play was unfinished; I heard another voice in my head and needed to let her speak. I'm glad she did because I like what came of the writing—if you look closely, you can also see bits and pieces that I've mined from this section and used elsewhere in the text. I suppose I liked the idea that our protagonist finds his journey changed along the way and returns to the geographical starting point—both of the play and his fictional life—to answer some questions that have long haunted him. The scene itself might even make a good one-act on its own for some ambitious theater company or college students; who knows, stranger things have happened.

In the end, *Some Girl(s)* was a treat to spend some time with again; I like all these folks enormously—even Guy, who (in the wrong hands) runs the risk of coming off as a self-serving, deceitful shithead. That may seem like a funny concern for a writer to have about one of his own creations, but I'm nothing if not honest about my fiction; life itself is a much trickier proposition, so if I'm not at least truthful about my fictional life, what chance do I have out there in the real world?

And hey, even self-serving, deceitful shitheads need some love on occasion—after all, they're just people, too.

Part __: "Reggie"

That hotel room again, refigured by somebody to have a more open, airy feel. Bigger windows. A softer color palette.

The man is standing at the door, just letting someone in. A girl of twenty-five or so—this one happens to be REGGIE—*enters into the room and stops, looking around at the pleasant surroundings. She fiddles with a large Starbucks cup in one hand.*

REGGIE . . . nice. Very nice. (*toward a painting*) I like the flamingos . . .

GUY Thanks.

REGGIE No, seriously, this is really nice. Big.

GUY Yeah, no, you're right—it's definitely big. Probably more than I needed, really, but . . .

REGGIE Hey, why not? Live a little . . .

GUY Exactly! (*smiles*) That's what I thought. I asked 'em for an upgrade this time, at the front desk.

REGGIE Yeah?

GUY Uh-huh. I figured what the hell, right? I've got one of those cards, those . . . you know, where you get points and all that crap; they accumulate each time you sleep over at one of their other resorts but, I mean, hey . . . when am I ever gonna visit *Bali* or someplace like that? Take a free weekend in Tonga . . . (*smiles*) I've been traveling so much throughout the states, though—lately, anyway—it's better if I at least enjoy the nights I do spend away from home . . . like this.

REGGIE Makes sense. (*Beat.*) Oh . . . but I thought you said you were getting married. On the phone you did.

GUY That's true, I did, yes . . .

REGGIE So, I mean . . . wouldn't it be good for that? A bridal suite or that sort of thing, down the road?

GUY No. (*Beat*.) See, no, because . . . we got the whole thing—the honeymoon package, I'm saying—from my in-laws. To be. My in-laws-to-be arranged this trip to Mexico, some hotel that they recommend and so, yes. That's what we're doing.

REGGIE Got it. (*smiles*) Then, yeah . . . an upgrade's perfect.

GUY I thought so. (*Beat*.) Corner room makes all the difference sometimes. A little balcony or whatever . . . terrace.

REGGIE I bet it does . . .

GUY Seriously.

REGGIE Well, however you did it . . . it's really very nice.

GUY Yep, I agree. Glad you like it. (*Beat*.) You're not . . . I mean, are you married or anything? I don't really . . .

REGGIE Uh-uh. I'm not anything . . . not yet.

They smile at each other and then drift into a kind of silence.

REGGIE I gotta say . . . I never expected to hear from you.

GUY No?

REGGIE Nope. Not really . . .

GUY Well, I'm . . . I was your brother's best friend. Kelly and I were always very close. In school, I'm saying.

REGGIE Not lately, though.

GUY No, that's true, not so much in the past . . .

REGGIE . . . fifteen years . . .

GUY Right! Not for a while, not for . . . yeah. A *decade* or so, but . . .

REGGIE I told him I was coming to see you, and he was knocked out by that. The idea that we were meeting, the two of us . . .

GUY Really? It's not so crazy. I mean, me being here in Seattle and everything . . . I don't get down to Dallas very often, if ever, so it'd be hard to, you know. Keep in touch with him.

REGGIE Yeah, but this is . . . it's not by happenstance or however they call it. Right? (*Beat.*) Is that a word, "happenstance"?

GUY I think so . . . or something like it. Very close to that.

REGGIE I believe that's right. "Happenstance."

GUY It could be . . .

REGGIE Well, you're the big-time writer . . .

GUY Ha! Teacher, really. I just . . . well, both. Now. I'm both now.

REGGIE Even worse. You should know better.

GUY I know, I know! I think that is it—"happenstance." Yeah.

REGGIE Anyhow, you're not here by that. Chance or anything— you're here in Seattle to see me, aren't you? Isn't that what you said?

GUY That's true . . . I did say that.

REGGIE Anyway, that's not what I told him . . . I fibbed a little.

GUY How's that?

REGGIE I told Kelly that you called me out of the blue . . .

GUY . . . which is true . . .

REGGIE Yes, but—anyway, I said you called me up, that you were in town for just the day and thought we should say hello, catch up on old times, grab a bite, et cetera. All that kinda stuff . . .

GUY Oh, I see. Got it.

REGGIE Which, of course, just made him ask more questions, like how'd you get my number, how come you hadn't called him in so long, et cetera. You know, "brother" crap.

GUY Sure, that's natural . . .

REGGIE Yeah. (*Beat.*) He said he'd wanted to talk to you ever since you did that story of yours, the magazine one that he read—he sent me a copy on my work fax, which got me totally busted—and I guess he even wrote you or something,

to your agent, maybe, but never heard anything back . . .
which bummed him out. A lot. (*Beat*.) He asked me to give
you this, anyway. Here. (*holds out a piece of folded paper*)
It's his work number and stuff . . .

REGGIE Thanks. I don't think . . . no, I would've seen it if he
ever . . .

REGGIE Doesn't matter. He was just surprised, is all.

GUY I'll check with my . . . maybe it got mixed in with a bunch
of other . . . (*Beat*.) I haven't been so great about keeping
up with everybody from school.

REGGIE No biggie. It's hard . . . I'm only twenty-six and it's
already hard. E-mail helps, but still . . .

GUY Yeah, e-mail's great for that. Quick note here and there.
(*Beat*.) 'S that what you are now? Twenty-*six*? Wow, time
just . . . you know.

REGGIE Yep. Flies . . .

GUY That's the one! (*makes a jet noise*) Whoosh!

A short laugh between them; Reggie takes a sip of her coffee.

GUY So . . . it's . . .

REGGIE You look a lot older.

GUY Yeah?

REGGIE Uh-huh.

GUY I suppose I do, sure. That long ago, I must . . . I mean, you
do, too, although not . . .

REGGIE Well, of course I do. Of course *I* would.

GUY Right . . .

REGGIE I was a kid. A child, really, but you were . . . I can
remember exactly what you looked like back then, *exactly*,
and I've always had that image in my head . . . of you, I
mean.

GUY I get it. Sure.

REGGIE And so for the last few days—and all the way over

here—I've been imagining you, but this younger guy that I knew back then. The guy that was always hanging out at our house and sleeping over and that stuff, et cetera.

GUY Uh-huh. (*Beat.*) I don't think you can use that right there . . .

REGGIE What's that?

GUY . . . nothing . . .

REGGIE No, what? What can't I use?

GUY Et cetera. I mean you *can*, of course—you can do whatever you want, I guess, that's the beauty of English!—but it's not proper.

REGGIE Why, what'd I say?

GUY Oh, I don't remember exactly, but when you were listing all that stuff—"sleeping over" and those other—you kept saying "and" between each thing, which is basically the same as using "et cetera" at the end. I mean, basically.

REGGIE Huh. (*Beat.*) You really are a teacher, aren't you?

GUY It's true . . . (*smiles*) Listen, you can say whatever you want. I'm sorry for even . . . it just gets to be habit.

REGGIE No problem. I get it. I do. (*Beat.*) Et cetera.

They share a smile this time—the man glances at his watch and Reggie catches him.

REGGIE I'm not keeping you from anything, am I?

GUY No, God, no . . .

REGGIE Good. That's good . . .

GUY I just . . . forgot the date, that's all. I've got a . . . whole . . .

REGGIE Oh. (*Beat.*) You're not really good at making stuff up, are you?

GUY Not really.

REGGIE Not for some man who makes his living doing it.

GUY Exactly! (*grins*) Yeah, that's something I should work on . . . my lying skills.

REGGIE They do come in handy!

GUY I know, I know! Okay, I'll put that on the list—although there's a few people out there who'd disagree with you! They'd say I'm a plenty good liar as it is . . .

REGGIE I bet . . . (*Beat.*) What "list"? You have a list?

GUY Sure. My to-do list. Self-improvement, that type of thing. Work out, read more, be a better friend . . .

REGGIE Et cetera. (*smiles*) See? I know how it works . . .

GUY Right! (*grins*) I had no doubt, Reggie. None at all.

REGGIE Good.

GUY Funny that, how we all ended up calling you Reggie . . .

REGGIE Not that funny . . . I mean, when your idiot parents go and name you *Regina*, what choice do you have?

GUY Ha! (*laughs*) It was a family name, wasn't it?

REGGIE Who cares?! It's just a nasty thing to do to your kids . . . shit like that. Imagine the *variations.*

GUY Oh, I think I've heard a few of 'em . . .

REGGIE I'm sure! Even *made* up a few, if I recall . . .

GUY . . . I stand before you an accused man . . .

REGGIE Not yet.

GUY What?

REGGIE Nothing. I'm kidding. (*smiles*) It's funny, though, that you mention a list, or putting that on your list . . .

GUY Yeah, why's that?

REGGIE . . . and then you call me like you did, just like that. (*snaps her fingers*) It's weird.

GUY Why? You've lost me here . . .

REGGIE I'm just . . . I was gonna call you, I guess. Or had thoughts about it at least, a few times over the years.

GUY . . . really?

REGGIE Sure—it was on my *list*, anyway . . . (*smiles*) To-do.

GUY Huh. How come?

REGGIE You know. (*Beat.*) Same reason you called me, probably.

GUY . . . I'm . . .

REGGIE Because of that one time.

GUY Oh. Are you . . . ? (*Beat.*) I mean, if you feel like we should . . .

REGGIE We never spoke about it and I didn't tell anybody and so I've just always wanted to, you know, clear the slate on that one . . . see if we could, I dunno, sort it out somehow.

GUY I understand. I do. I really do understand . . .

REGGIE *Don't* say that—don't go on about "understanding" me about it, okay, because . . . that makes it seem like it was me who brought it up and you're surprised by the whole thing. Taken aback. Et cetera. (*Beat.*) It is why you contacted me, right? Yes?

GUY . . . yeah. It's something that . . . yes, Reggie.

REGGIE Okay, then.

The man moves over to the minifridge and looks inside. Gets a bottle of water for himself.

GUY Anything?

REGGIE I'd take a beer if they have it . . .

GUY Ummm, sure. It's . . . Coors Lite or Bud. It's a pretty generic selection, I'm afraid.

REGGIE Bud. I like Stella, but Bud is fine.

The man nods, snags a bottle and brings it to REGGIE. *Opens it on the way over. She smiles and takes it as she sets her Starbucks cup down. Gulps down some hops and grains.*

REGGIE Wow. Super-cold.

GUY Hope that's okay . . .

REGGIE Hey, I'm not English. I've turned out to be a pretty complicated girl, but at least I don't drink *warm* beer . . .

GUY Right! No wonder they colonized the world . . . "Some ice, some ice, my kingdom for some ice!" (*Beat.*) Sorry, that was dumb . . .

REGGIE No, I just don't get it . . . what's it from?

GUY Oh, ahhh . . . *Richard III.* Shakespeare.

REGGIE I got that part. I'm not retarded . . .

GUY Of course not! I didn't mean . . .

REGGIE I'm kidding. I'm pretty retarded in terms of crap like that. Trivial Pursuit and that sorta junk . . . (*Beat.*) It's a quote, right?

GUY Yeah . . . "A horse, a horse, my kingdom for a horse!"

REGGIE Right, right, yeah, I've heard that one. Shakespeare.

GUY Exactly . . .

REGGIE Huh. So, why's he want one so badly? A horse, I mean?

GUY Oh, he's, ummm . . . you know. He's about to get killed because, for all the bad stuff he's done. So he's trying to escape . . .

REGGIE Ha! How appropriate! (*laughs*) That's a good one . . .

GUY . . . I'm lost. What're you . . . ?

REGGIE If you don't get it, then don't worry about it. (*Beat.*) You guys used to play that all the time, remember? Trivial Pursuit. You and Kelly would sit down in the basement for *hours* doing that thing, with all those little colored chips . . . (*laughs*) My dad used to call it "Frivolous Pursuit," you remember?

GUY Oh, yeah! (*grins*) Pie pieces. That's what they were called. The little wedges of, ahhh . . .

REGGIE Whatever. You two would do that downstairs and my mom'd scream her head off every Friday when she was vacuuming down there and she'd get five or six of 'em jammed into her Hoover . . . she hardly ever used to yell or anything—my mom, I mean—but for some reason that really bugged the shit outta her. Those little bits of plastic getting swallowed up in her hose . . .

GUY I remember that. Sure.

REGGIE Yep. And you'd go running back home to your place, anytime she'd start up at Kelly . . . he always had to just stay there and take it, but I noticed that you would disappear . . . I was only, like, little at the time, but I noticed that.

GUY I probably did, you're right . . . I never liked to get in the middle of family stuff like that. Even at my house, I'd take off outside or go down to the school. (*Beat.*) Conflict's not, like, my favorite thing.

REGGIE Yeah, I can see that. I mean, it's there in your writing, too . . .

GUY Oh. I mean, huh. So, you've read the . . . ?

REGGIE The fax, remember? Kelly got me in trouble, I had to at least read the damn thing!

GUY Right!

REGGIE Your character in that . . . all those run-ins with women and his big defense is to slip away. Get out through the window, et cetera. Whatever it takes to save his own skin . . .

GUY Right, but . . . mostly it's for comic effect. Irony and all that. The, ahh, repetition of a motif—the hasty exit—is a classic sort of . . . umm . . .

REGGIE Still . . . I don't figure you made it all up.

GUY Mostly I did. It's . . . satire. A send-up of sexual politics and based on *Candide*, as well . . . it's, ahhh . . . anyhow, doesn't matter.

REGGIE No? So, then, it's all just this big . . . fantasy?

GUY Well, I mean, *certain* episodes—an incident or a phrase, that kind of thing—can't help but seep in, but . . . yes, it's from the imagination. Mostly.

REGGIE Got it. (*smiles*) Whatever you say, Shakespeare . . .

GUY "Shakespeare." Ha! That's a good one . . .

REGGIE Well, you always did want to be a writer, didn't you?

GUY I think so . . . in some way, yes I did. Yeah. (*Beat.*) You can't possibly remember that, though. No way!

REGGIE You'd be surprised. I remember a lot of stuff . . .

GUY Sure, but . . .

REGGIE I used to watch you—you were my favorite of Kelly's friends and so, yeah, I used to follow you guys around, spy on you and all that crap. I overheard a *bunch*, things you wouldn't even remember now . . .

GUY Oh, yeah?

REGGIE Sure . . . I was stealthy. A regular little Mata Hari.

GUY Well, don't forget what happened to her . . .

REGGIE Why, you gonna shoot me?

GUY Oh, I don't know—is that how she died? I have no idea, I was just saying that . . .

REGGIE Really?

GUY Yeah. I mean, yes, I think I do recall that she was killed or something, executed for being a, you know . . . spy.

REGGIE Uh-huh. But a sexy one . . .

GUY True.

REGGIE Like me. (*grins*) I turned out kinda sexy, don't you think? I mean, objectively speaking and all . . .

GUY Ummm . . .

REGGIE Damn, come on! Give a girl some credit here . . .

GUY Of course you are, Reggie. Of course. It's just . . .

REGGIE What?

GUY You're my friend's little sister . . . Kelly's *sis.* So . . .

REGGIE Never stopped you before.

GUY . . . look . . .

REGGIE I'm just saying . . .

GUY I know, but . . . (*Beat.*) Anyway, yes, you've turned out to be a very beautiful woman, but you're not just some gal here. You and I are . . . we're . . .

REGGIE Connected?

GUY No, I was gonna say . . . I mean, yes, we are, yeah. Grew up together, the same neighborhood and all, but . . .

REGGIE Anyhow, the point was that I liked you best of Kelly's pals and I really did overhear a bunch of crap that you guys said to each other . . . no joke.

GUY Like what?

REGGIE Ummm . . . stuff about classes, giving each other the answers for tests and jokes that you heard from people, people that he or you liked. I heard you tell him that you were gonna break up with what's-her-name and how there was a girl, some girl at another school that you had the hots for . . . shit like that.

GUY Oh. Huh. (*Beat.*) That's . . .

REGGIE Am I even close?

GUY Yeah, not too bad . . . you little snoop!

REGGIE Ha! (*grins*) What else're you gonna do when you're that age?

GUY Watch *cartoons* or something! (*laughs*) So, you said that you were thinking about getting ahold of me . . .

REGGIE Yep. That's right . . .

GUY How come? Seriously . . .

REGGIE You know . . . right? I mean . . .

GUY I guess, but, it's . . . why now? So much later in life . . .

REGGIE Just 'cause. (*Beat.*) Actually, I wrote it in my journal— I never spoke to anybody about it, *no* one—and I promised that I'd give it fifteen years for you to ask me to marry you, and if you hadn't done it in that amount of time, then I was gonna tell on you . . . say something to somebody, at least. My mom, maybe.

GUY Really?

REGGIE Something like that! I don't remember how I worded it exactly, but some sort of crazy statement along those lines. Yep. (*Beat.*) Hey, I was a kid, what can I say?

GUY Wow . . . that's, you know . . . (*Beat.*) I never knew that you kept a journal. At *eleven?*

REGGIE Uh-huh. I wanted to be a writer, too . . . because of you.

GUY . . . no . . .

REGGIE It's true.

GUY And you . . . I mean, isn't that what you do now? Or . . .

REGGIE Sort of. Journalist, anyway, but mostly freelance . . .

GUY Still, that's . . .

REGGIE It's whatever. Pays the bills. I do human interest stories and that kind of thing. Stories like ours . . .

GUY What do you mean?

REGGIE Nothing. I mean, I'd never do it, but this'd make a hell of an article, us meeting again, after all this time . . . what you ended up doing, and me, how things affected me, who I turned out to be. That sort of deal. (*Beat.*) Like you did with that story of yours, but without all the—what'd you call 'em?—*motifs.*

GUY Reggie, listen, I never . . . I think maybe we should talk.

REGGIE We are. We're doing that right now. Talking.

GUY I know, but . . .

REGGIE Just like I promised we would, in my journal . . .

GUY Uh-huh, right, but . . .

REGGIE I gotta tell you, you just made it under the wire! (*laughs*) Almost to the day . . .

GUY How's that?

REGGIE The date of that entry, I remember it because it was my birthday. You might not know that, but it happened the night you slept over, on my twelfth birthday, because Mom wanted Kelly to have you stay with us so he wouldn't bug us girls during my party . . . that's the night it happened. *Us.*

GUY All that we . . . I mean, it was just a kiss. That's all.

REGGIE That's *all*?

GUY . . . yes . . .

REGGIE . . . I was twelve. Not even, 'cause it was before midnight.

GUY I know, but . . .

REGGIE I can't help it. I'm a journalist, so I stick pretty close to the facts . . .

GUY No, I get it, I do, I'm just saying . . .

REGGIE What? What'd you wanna add to that?

GUY Just that I didn't . . . you know, I never . . .

REGGIE No, what?

GUY I didn't mean anything by it.

REGGIE Oh.

GUY I mean, not that it wasn't good, or . . .

REGGIE You enjoyed it?

GUY . . . no, but . . .

REGGIE You didn't? (*Beat.*) I did.

GUY I mean, no, I didn't enjoy it, like, in some *sexual* way or whatnot, but of course it was nice, of course it was . . .

REGGIE It *was* nice, huh?

GUY Yes. Nice, and tender and, ummm . . . sweet . . .

REGGIE Et cetera.

GUY Yeah, right. Et cetera.

REGGIE Did I use it okay that time?

GUY . . . I'm trying to be serious here.

REGGIE Me, too. I'm being totally serious right now. (*Beat.*) And that's how you remember it? Just like that? "Sweet . . ."

GUY Mostly. It was . . . I mean, it only lasted a few . . .

REGGIE It was a kiss. A *full* kiss on my mouth. My twelve-year-old mouth . . . eleven, technically. I was still eleven.

GUY I know that.

REGGIE Good. I'm glad . . . (*Beat.*) And what else?

GUY "Else"? What do you mean?

REGGIE I mean what else happened? I want to see if our stories jibe so that I can then close the book on this and move on with my life . . . not that it was this *major* deal, but still . . .

GUY Reggie . . . I'm very . . .

REGGIE What else do you remember? (*Beat.*) You made it in on the time-limit thing, but I'm still mulling over the story deal or talking to somebody else—my mom, or *Kelly*—so it's up to you . . .

GUY Please don't do that.

REGGIE I need some closure.

GUY Fine. Then let's . . . fine. I'll . . . just don't do that.

REGGIE Tell me then . . .

GUY We . . . God, it's been so long that I . . . I guess that
we . . .

REGGIE Why're you here? Tell me that. Why did you come to
Seattle and call me up? I don't get it . . .

GUY I was . . . I dunno, I felt like I wanted to . . .

REGGIE What? What did you want?

GUY Or needed to, maybe . . . I needed to get this off of my
chest with you. Before I get married and everything, I
wanted to talk about things and just, you know . . . say,
"Hey, I know this happened and all and I still think about it,
play around with it in my head so she must, too, so we
oughta . . ." That's about as far as it ever goes, but I do
weigh it out every so often. I do, Reggie . . .

REGGIE Good. Well, that's good to hear . . .

GUY And I was—this is the truth—I was in town recently, a few
days ago, seeing my, umm . . . this *conference* thingie I
attended . . . and I happened to see you. Just crossing the
street in front of me, like something out of a movie, or . . .
(*Beat*.) Remember the way that Janet Leigh's boss in *Psycho*
strolls right in front of her car after she stole all that money
from the bank and he looks at her—there's a whole weird
moment there—but he just keeps on walking . . . we had one
of those. I mean, I don't know if you saw me—or that film,
even!—but it was just like that on my side. I'm in this little
rented Ford Focus and suddenly there you are in front of me
in the crosswalk, carrying a *Starbucks* cup and talking on
your cell. Fifteen years later and I had no doubt, *none*, that it
was you . . . (*Beat*.) I flew outta town the next afternoon,
but it kept gnawing at me—that image of you in the middle
of the street there—so I tracked you down in the white
pages, found you and called. I left that message on your
machine . . .

REGGIE That's funny. I didn't even notice you . . .

GUY It didn't seem like you did, but I couldn't stop thinking
about it . . .

REGGIE . . . and so you called. You rang me up.

GUY Yeah. Called and flew back here so that we could . . . whatever. So that we might have a moment like this one. Or . . .

REGGIE I get it. (*Beat.*) Do you remember touching my ass?

GUY . . . no. I don't, Reggie. Honestly. No.

REGGIE Because you did . . . (*laughs*) I didn't even know I had one of those back then—it was just my little ol' behind, something that my daddy would pinch and my mother would pat and . . . whatever. Et cetera. But that night, when everybody else was asleep—my friends, anyhow, I think Kelly had snuck off to try and get you guys some beer from our neighbors' garage, they had a fridge that they kept out there—you and I were . . . we were both in the kitchen and we were laughing about, I don't know what—you were probably making fun of me, like usual!—and somehow, I mean, you were suddenly just right there, in my face, and I was scared but I didn't leave, I didn't pull away or anything; it was like a truth or dare or something, like in spin the bottle. No big deal. But then . . .

GUY . . . I kissed you.

REGGIE Yes. We kissed. We kissed and I . . . grew up, right there. Instantly. I became like this . . . suddenly I was *aware* of things. Of *me*. And I kissed you back, only for a few moments, but we were doing it like some couple. We were kissing and you whispered, "I'm gonna marry you someday." You did. You said that to me and then . . . then I felt your hand on me, down on my . . . in my . . .

GUY . . . I didn't mean to, Reggie, I really didn't . . .

REGGIE Your hand was there, slipping into my panties and I was . . . you made me all . . . (*starts to tear up*) . . . that was too much! You did that and I looked at you—I can remember looking right into those beautiful eyes of yours—and I . . . I ran away. Back up to my friends, all my sleeping friends who

AFTERWORD(S)

were still just young girls, some girls that I was never gonna be like again. Not ever.

GUY I'm . . . Jesus, Reggie, I am so, *so* sorry if you . . . you feel like I'm responsible for . . .

REGGIE What? "Responsible" for what?

GUY I dunno. I didn't really get to the end of that thought . . . I figured I should just get it out there while the going's good. (*Beat*.) I'm trying to be honest here . . . I really, really am.

REGGIE At least you're funny . . . sort of. You were always funny.

GUY Thanks . . . that's a very . . . thank you.

REGGIE *nods and turns away, wiping at her eyes. The man sits on the bed and waits. It's definitely her move.*

GUY We were just . . . it's okay. I think. I mean, yes, we probably shouldn't've done it, let it happen, but we're, you know . . . we were just kids.

REGGIE No, don't say that! Do not say it that way. "Kids."

GUY What do you mean?

REGGIE I was a kid. Me, I was . . . a little girl, but you weren't. You were not a child at all. Uh-uh. You were eighteen . . .

GUY No, I was . . . this was . . .

REGGIE October. Twenty-third of October, remember? My birthday . . . three days from *now* . . .

GUY . . . right . . . (*checks his watch again*) Of course.

REGGIE Your birthday's in August. I looked it up because I couldn't recall it, and it's August. Seventh. You were already eighteen.

GUY Okay, fine, yes . . . that's true, but . . .

REGGIE But what? (*Beat*.) You were a man, doesn't matter how you wanna spin it—you could vote, go to war, had a car and all . . . you had no business doing that with me. Not that night or ever.

GUY Reggie, you're . . . no, you're right. I didn't realize that you . . .

REGGIE I'm not gonna lay the whole "you ruined my life" dish on you because I'm not even sure that's true . . . I am who I am, who I turned out to be or whatever, but you had some part in it, I guess that's all I wanted you to know . . . your doing that—to me, on that night—had something to do with this . . . what you see before you. (*Beat.*) Cute, smart, hardworking, kinda fucked up, sexually inappropriate at a pretty early age, just making it some days and other times off the charts and laser sharp . . . *et cetera.* (*smiles*) Just thought you should know, that's all.

GUY I'm . . . God, I'm so . . .

REGGIE I don't really still expect you to marry me, by the way. That part was a little bit silly . . . even back then.

GUY Reggie . . .

REGGIE I should get going . . . there's always traffic around here these days. (*points to her cup*) Thanks to these bastards!

GUY Right . . . (*grins*) I suppose so.

REGGIE Most of us are really—people, I mean—we're basically to blame for our own shit, I really do believe that. I guess I just needed to tell somebody about it. You and me. Share it with another person for a second . . . what happened there. How it, you know, affected me. (*Beat.*) It was just too much for a kid to handle all on her own . . . I mean, it's a kiss, right? Just a *kiss.* Get over it! But it's hard . . . it's just so damn hard to . . . I dunno. Let it go, I s'pose. To let go . . .

GUY I get that, I do, and I'm glad you did. Truthfully.

REGGIE Yeah?

GUY Yes.

REGGIE Okay, then . . . (*makes a gesture*) . . . it's off the list.

They smile at each other briefly, then return to silence. REGGIE *stands up and moves toward the door. The man follows her.*

Without warning, REGGIE *grabs and pushes him up against the door, looking deeply into his eyes. Dead quiet. After a moment, she kisses him. Long and hard. He responds.*

REGGIE There. *That's* what a woman kisses like . . . see the
    difference?
GUY Yes. I do, yeah . . .
REGGIE . . . then good.

Without another word, REGGIE *goes to the door and opens it. Disappears down the hallway. The man watches her go, slowly closing the door after a long while.*

He crosses to the bed and sits. Breathing heavily in and out.